CULTURE TO CATWALK

HOW WORLD CULTURES INFLUENCE FASHION

First published in 2011 by A & C Black,
an imprint of Bloomsbury Publishing Plc.
49-51 Bedford Square,
London WC1B 3DP

www.acblack.com

CIP Catalogue records for this book are available
from the British Library and the US Library of
Congress.

Publisher: Susan James
Project Editor: Ellen Parnavelas
Copy Editor: Julian Beecroft
Book design by Evelin Kasikov
Cover design by James Watson
Captions by Paul James Lynch

All images provided by Getty Images

ISBN 978-1-4081-3071-1

This book is produced using paper that is made
from wood grown in managed, sustainable
forests. It is natural, renewable and recyclable.
The logging and manufacturing processes
conform to the environmental regulations of
the country of origin.

Cover Images
Front: A model walks the runway during the Kenzo
Ready to Wear Spring/Summer 2011 show during
Paris Fashion Week. Provided by Getty Images.
Back: Model walks the runway for Elie Saab
Spring/Summer 2010, Paris Fashion Week Haute
Couture. Provided by Getty Images.
Front Flap: Portrait of the author by
Adrian Morales

Additional Image Credits
Background image pp. 2, 6–7
Examples of Indian textiles used to make a sari,
the traditional Indian woman's garment

Background image pp. 4–5
Women dressed in traditional Mexican costume
Background image pp. 8–9
A t-shirt with a portrait of Che Guevara
Background image pp. 10–11
Babouches (Moroccan slippers) on sale
in the medina. Marrakech, Morocco

Background image pp. 254–256
Gold Indian bangles on purple sari cloth

All provided by Getty Images.

Printed and bound in China.

CULTURE TO CATWALK

HOW WORLD CULTURES INFLUENCE FASHION

kristin knox

Contents

asia

the americas

Introduction

'The garment is a ghost of all the multiple lives it may have had. Nothing is shiny and new; everything has a history… The design is a wish or a curse that casts the garment and its wearer into a time warp through historical periods, like a sudden tumble through the sediment of an archaeological dig.' Thus wrote Turkish-born avant-garde designer Hussein Chalayan in the show notes to Medea, his Spring/Summer 2002 runway show.

Fashion designers have been playing on this notion in their work since the inception of what we think of as the ready-to-wear industry, with industrialization, in the 19th century. Clothing, and the way we make our clothing, is a reflection of who we are as human beings, culturally and socially. But what Hussein Chalayan here glosses over is that the garment at the hands of a fashion designer is not only a time-traveller, but also a globetrotter, a vagabond who travels the world over and back again to the atelier. There is hardly a fashion designer out there who has not, at some point in his or her career, claimed 'culture X' or 'civilization Y' as inspiration for at least one of their catwalk collections. In fact, some, like Vivienne Tam, with her East-meets-West tailored sensibilities, or Hussein Chalayan, with his conceptual politics, or John Galliano, with his worldly theatrics, have made a career out of playing with other cultures.

Culture and fashion have always been inexplicably intertwined, the clash of East and West, the interplay of different textiles, colour palettes, beading, embroidery and other culturally specific crafts with Western sartorial traditions, pattern-cutting and tailoring: in the interaction of the two lies innovation in design. Simultaneous with the birth of ready-to-wear came a renewed European interest in the Near and Far East, Africa and Latin America, as the West sought to use technology to expand its borders, an interest which was felt across art, architecture and in the budding fashion industry.

Paul Poiret, who established his house in 1903, for example, made his name as a designer after he turned the Japanese kimono into a coat for the Parisiennes willing to take a chance on something new. The kimono wraparound shape has been integral to fashion design ever since. The Algerian-born Yves Saint Laurent years later, in 1967, showed a collection inspired by African art, and 50 years later,

for the Spring/Summer 2009 season, African and tribal influences would once again become a major seasonal trend, manifesting itself in the form of African prints, textiles, beading and more.

It is also worth noting the obvious point that fashion designers also come from all over the world, but historically have set up their ateliers in Paris or Milan or another Western fashion capital. Thus, though a designer may be Chinese or Colombian, they are subsumed by the runway culture of Europe and America, and often fuse their own national or regional design instincts and cultural nuances within the accepted sartorial practices of the West.

This book, first and foremost, explores this phenomenon in recent fashion history, seeking to highlight the key items of traditional global dress and national costume from parts of Asia, Africa, the Middle East and Latin America that have most influenced the great fashion designers of the Western fashion world. As designers are often as astute in their historical research as they are in their cutting and sewing, historical and cultural references are often not without meaning. Designers study the politics and the discourse behind a certain kind of dress, learning everything they can about the man or woman who would have worn the garment, how his or her world may have differed from ours, and then exploit the fact. Therefore, in order to fully appreciate the exoticism and sometimes even the political undercurrents of many an 'ethnically inspired' fashion collection, it is crucial to have at least some basic fashion anthropology, as most designers do.

The second aim of this book is to look at global fashion today, the backswing against the Eurocentricity that has governed the fashion industry since the 19th century. Over the years, as we moved further and further away from the original houses of the time when orientalism flourished in the arts, with increasing globalization in general came the globalization of fashion and a ubiquitous norm dictated by trends coming out of Milan, Paris, London, New York and perhaps Tokyo. All one has to do to paint a clear picture is utter the words, 'jeans and t-shirts'. Perhaps it would always have been were it not that these things are cyclical, that politics and economics shift and the world changes and grows. And fashion, after all, is a business. So as countries like China and India become more prominent players in the global economy, a desire to nurture a local fashion industry eventually develops on the ground in these places. Accordingly, fashion weeks have sprung up all over the world, negating the need for young designers to flock to the fashion capitals of Europe in order to 'make it'. Local governments from places as different as Brazil and Pakistan are investing in local textile and garment industries, hoping to foster a uniquely national, autonomous fashion industry.

This shift in global power, coupled with the birth of the internet, I would argue, has shifted the focus back to what people are wearing locally, and fashion designers are once again looking to cultural pockets and individuals from far-flung corners of the world for inspiration for their catwalk collections. To see this in action we need look no further than Paul Smith's Spring/Summer 2010 collection, which transformed the poverty-stricken dandies of the Congo, the *Sapeurs*, into a strong runway statement at London Fashion Week. Fashion has always been and will always be just another manifestation of our shared global heritage as human beings.

Lastly, this book is concerned with a third and final piece of the puzzle. The zeitgeist has come full circle and the concept of 'street style' once again has designers looking at what people are actually wearing around the world as creative inspiration for their collections. The rise of the idea of street style, the power of individuality to stand out against the grain, has re-emerged in the collective consciousness of mainstream youth and spread fast. With the rapidly growing popularity of street-style blogs and even glossy magazines now featuring street style –cool kids captured in their natural habitat as opposed to models stylised in studio photo shoots. Suddenly, it is the 'real' element, the human element, that becomes cool, just as it was when Paul Poiret first introduced the kimono to the corseted and bustled ladies of turn-of-the-century Paris.

Individuality has once again become a creative commodity, and young, ultra-hip designers and brands like Alexander Wang and Marc Jacobs are increasingly looking to street cool from all over the world to influence and breathe new life into their catwalk shows. Marc Jacobs told *Vogue*'s Emma Elwick in 2010 that his Spring/Summer 2010 collection for Louis Vuitton was inspired by 'things that are an everyday pedestrian part of the urban landscape'. He continued by describing the person

> *'Street garment finishes have been creeping into couture with raw edges, 'rough' finishes and new fabrics, that years ago would never have been used in couture garments.'*

for whom the collection is designed – in essence, the logged-on youth of today. 'We wanted to reinterpret them and put them together with a kind of new age traveller in mind … They embrace punk, hippie and many other cultures, as well as cyber. So it was a mix that was non-ethnic but totally ethnic at the same time: a mix of cultures, street terminology and slang.'

Much-loved British designer Zandra Rhodes concurs that the influence of 'street' is palpable in high fashion, going even so far as to admit that it has infiltrated the highest compendium of fashion design, couture. 'Street garment finishes have been creeping into couture with raw edges, "rough" finishes and new fabrics that years ago would never have been used in couture garments.' Culture, now 'street' culture, has once again influenced the catwalk. The power to influence and manipulate the zeitgeist lies in the unique and the eccentric, as opposed to the uniform and conformist. So once again the clash of cultures and identities, as it can express itself through fashion, has moved centre stage.

On the flip side, beyond Paris and New York the internet also allows us glimpses into fashion communities around the world previously unknown to the average fashionista. Countries without a *Vogue*, without glossy publications, found themselves losing their young design talents to the so-called capitals, where their work had a better chance of being seen. But with the advent of blogs and social media, low-cost platforms have encouraged local talent to try again in their own backyard.

'Emerging Indonesian designers are definitely a force we can't leave behind, as they already have such a huge following. Since they are young, they use technology in their day-to-day life, so it helps them in promoting their designs,' explains Hanifa Ambadar, Editor-in-Chief of *Fashionese Daily*, Indonesia's premier fashion blog, launched in 2005. 'They have used Twitter, Facebook, websites and other media to gain followers.'

It's not just happening in Southeast Asia, but all over the world, from Morocco to Mexico to Madagascar. More and more fashionably minded individuals are scrambling to put their national sartorial heritage and budding fashion stars on the international digital map–a very recent phenomenon in those parts of the world that have only recently come online. As Nigerian blogger Terence Sambo recounts, 'Up until 2007 I had no idea blogs existed or what they were, as the internet was still elusive in most parts of Africa...I launched my first blog, a menswear global blog, in 2008, born out of the need to show the world what Nigerian and African fashion and style was all about.' Even established American designer Zac Posen, during an interview with the author for the *Daily Mail* in February 2011, had to concede with regard to the internet's debut influence on fashion, 'the game has changed'.

So to return to Hussein Chalayan's notion of the garment as a 'ghost of multiple lives', we see that, in fact, the ghost is no more than our own shadow, mimicking our own actions and following us wherever we go. And as far as fashion creativity is concerned, this ghost is not one we should ever try to exorcise. Culture and the catwalk are inextricably bound up in one another, always have been and always will be, though the form in which they interact may change from one era to the next. Fashion, like human society, is a global affair. And whether Paris, Milan, New York and London remain the main centres of gravity or these centres weaken, to be replaced instead by 100 smaller local fashion weeks dotting the globe, that ongoing evolution and dialogue provoked by the interaction of different cultures, provocative or otherwise, is what will continue helping fashion to amount to more than just the clothes.

Author's note

This book is first and foremost an adaptation of *The Berg Encyclopedia of World Dress and Fashion*, first published in 2010. The original ten-volume set served as both the template for the roster of countries featured in *Culture to Catwalk* and the infrastructure for its chapters and their contents. *The Berg Encyclopedia of World Dress and Fashion* also served as the primary historical and anthropological source for this book.

A number of interviews were conducted with members of the fashion industry for the purposes of this book, and these are quoted throughout. All quotations used are from these direct interviews unless otherwise stated. Other sources used for research include contemporary materials available online, such as archive runway reviews and also newer media including blogs from around the world.

Unlike its source text, the purpose of this book is not to offer an academically comprehensive survey of everything included under the term 'world fashion', but rather to scratch the surface of an exciting and largely overlooked facet of the fashion industry, i.e. the cross-cultural discourse that lies at the heart of fashion design and innovation. World fashion is a global dialogue, and this book is meant to be a prompt to that conversation, not to present itself as a final word on the subject. My hope is that the book will inspire students and lovers of fashion alike to look further afield than the catwalks and fashion histories of Paris, Milan, London and New York, and to show that everywhere there is culture there can be a catwalk. Ideally, this book will spawn 50 more on the topic, each more specialized than the last, as the field of global fashion is as broad as the world is wide and the history of human beings is long.

africa

Introduction

Scientists trace the origin of the human species to the African continent, specifically to the region occupied by the modern countries of Tanzania, Kenya and Ethiopia. As *Homo Sapiens* evolved, they eventually learned to clothe themselves, thus making Africa not only the cradle of humanity, but also the birthplace of fashion.

'Fast-forward many years, and time and time again we have seen the evidence of many West African-inspired collections, prints and trends.'

Given its seminal place in the human story, perhaps it is no wonder that Africa's sartorial tradition at home and its influence abroad is as diverse and eclectic as the continent is vast. Flowing robes with richly embroidered patterns, cloth dyed or printed in brilliant colours, towering head ties and turbans, profusions of beaded bracelets and necklaces – these and many other elements of African dress associated with both tribal and colonial cultures have come out of Africa and onto the catwalks of Europe. Even forms as basic to our dress repertoire as the strapless dress can be seen as evolving out of Africa. 'Most strapless and single-strap dresses originated from traditional West African ways of dressing,' says Mabel Kwei, renowned lecturer in art history and design and former Head of the Art Department at Gambia College, West Africa. 'The African teenage girl will just pick up a piece of fabric about two yards long and just tie it around her chest, covering her breast, and go everywhere with it all day. So will a boy use the same piece to tie around his neck and do everything with it.'

Yves Saint Laurent famously took an African theme for his Spring 1968 collection and, in addition to dressing African models in fringed, woven and beaded raffia dresses, that collection also saw the dawn of the iconic 'safari' suit, transforming the

Opposite Oscar de la Renta Spring/Summer 2008

classic men's garb of the African colonial era into chic, sexy urbanwear. The influences of the Algerian-born Saint Laurent's safari look are too many to count, but the trend enjoyed a particular resurgence after the designer's passing in 2008. Rag & Bone, Oscar de la Renta, Michael Kors, Jean Paul Gaultier, Elie Tahari, Chaiken, Hermès and Diane von Fürstenberg all referenced the safari in their Spring/Summer 2008 collections in homage to the late designer.

'Fast-forward many years, and time and time again we have seen the evidence of many West African-inspired collections, prints and trends. For Spring/Summer 2010 one of the most prominent trends is the Ethnic/Tribal trend,' states London-based Ghanaian-born celebrity stylist and blogger (and daughter of Kwei) Marian Kihogo. 'The likes of renowned Belgian fashion designers showed prints inspired by ethnic West Africa. Influence from this part of the world was also seen in Jean Paul Gaultier's Autumn/Winter 2010–11 show, with his models in West African-inspired head wraps.'

Indeed, taking up this tribal theme Dolce and Gabbana kicked off their Spring/Summer 2005 show with model Naomi Campbell clad in a reptilian corset dress, her arms and neck piled up with beaded and intricate metal tribal jewellery. For Spring/Summer 2007, New York-based designer Alexandre Herchcovitch's collection was inspired by the Ndebele tribe of Zimbabwe, who are known for their brightly coloured houses and elaborate beadwork. French designer Christian Lacroix, known for his love of vibrant colours, is also an Africa enthusiast. Spring/Summer 2009 also saw a surge of African influence on the catwalk, tribalism

Naomi Campbell wears African inspired Dolce & Gabbana at Milan fashion week Spring/Summer 2005

Oscar de la Renta Spring/Summer 2008

Top Bright *Kente* cloth from eastern Ghana

Bottom left Maasai women dressed in traditional clothing

Bottom right Male member of the Turkana tribe wearing traditional bright fabric

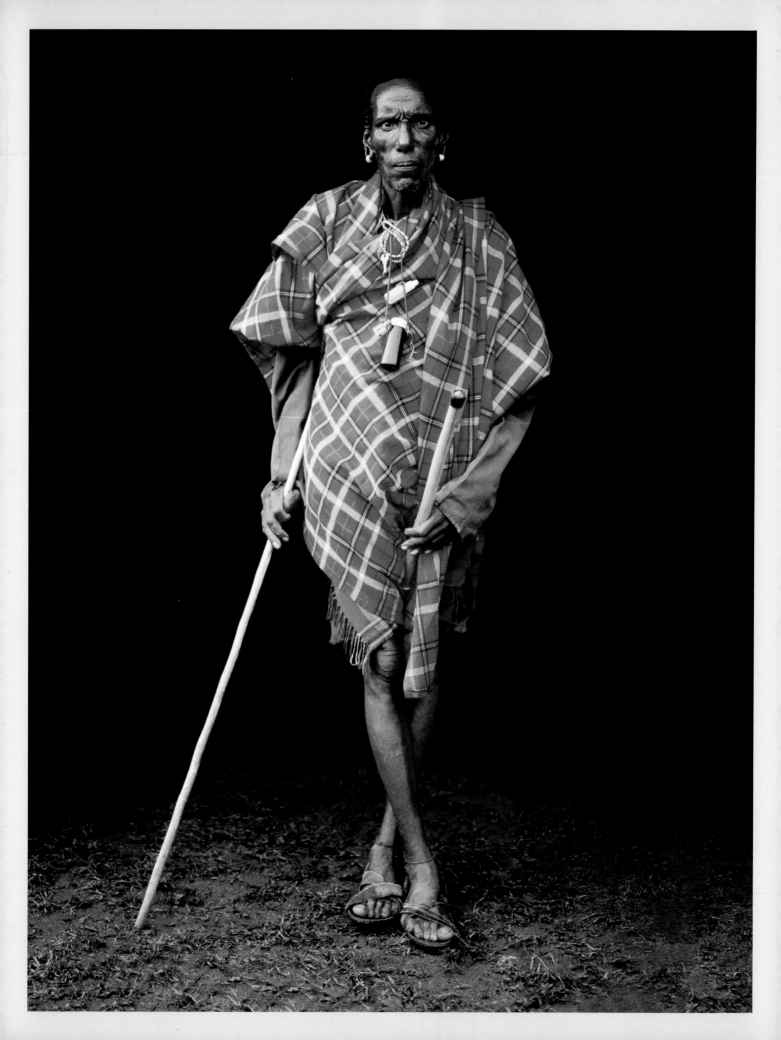

Opposite Samburu Tribal Elder dressed in bright check fabric

Top left A Maasai warrior wearing traditional beading

Top right Beading of the Turkana tribe in Northern Kenya

Bottom Tribal jewellery at Louis Vuitton, Paris Fashion Week Spring/Summer 2009

being pegged as one of the season's key trends, largely due to the method of styling.

"The vibrant colour palette of African prints and way of life as whole informs my wardrobe and even my styling wardrobe," points out Marian Kihogo. "It helps me see and employ colour, fabric, print, draping and embellishment in a different light." Indeed, this is the light in which Junya Watanabe must have basked as he sent girls down the runway in Paris sporting towering head wraps and dresses fashioned from twisted, draped, bunched and layered yards of fabric rendered in an amalgam of African prints interspersed with bright gingham check and flashes of neon. Diane von Furstenberg reworks brightly coloured, printed Moroccan-style kaftans, and Christopher Kane screenprinted angry gorillas onto sculpted dresses. Marc Jacobs created his iconic, bestselling tribal shoes for Louis Vuitton in 2009 and, the following season, turned out a collection rife with African-inspired prints for his own eponymous line.

Model wears African print dress at Diane von Furstenberg Spring/Summer 2008

Model wears African inspired Kaftan at Diane von Furstenberg Spring/Summer 2008

Tribal shoes by Marc Jacobs for Louis Vuitton, Paris Fashion Week Fall 2008

Top left Model walks the runway at the Arise Magazine African Collection in New York, Fall 2010

Top right A model presents a creation by French designer Catherine Bizoux at the International Festival of African Fashion

Bottom A model presents a creation by French designer Catherine Bizoux at the International Festival of African Fashion

Local fashion design in Africa itself is still an emerging industry. There is no intrinsically African style that can be applied to such a diverse continent. Yet common themes and concerns traverse the collections of many African designers. Some focus on achieving a modern hybridization of Western styles rendered in local fabrics, such as a man's suit with lapels made of cloth produced locally or a woman's miniskirt adorned with beadwork in a style associated with indigenous dress. Others look more to the conceptual side of fashion design to help express political or social concerns and beliefs, using fashion as an artistic outlet for self-expression; their references are conceptual rather than literal, making no direct visual reference to the forms and materials usually associated with African cultures.

The first generation of African designers came of age after the Second World War, just as the struggle for African independence from European colonial rule was beginning to achieve its aims across the continent. Fashion has only been a formal profession there since the 1970s. Several designers who have been credited with establishing contemporary African fashion design were part of this first generation. Chris Seydou, Alphadi, Kofi Ansah, and Michael Kra were all instrumental in the creation of an African fashion-design movement, through both their own success as designers and entrepreneurs and their efforts in championing African design abroad. Led by Chris Seydou, these men were among the group of designers who created the Fédération Africaine des Créateurs in 1993, the first transnational organization of African fashion designers.

Not surprisingly, much of the work of those African fashion designers whose sensibilities were informed by the political mood of this period reflects a desire to bring African styles to global fashion markets. Most studied and worked in Europe or the United States, through which they introduced the techniques and styles of international fashion to their work in Africa.

Fashion in Africa today emerges out of the continent's long creative history and, like the globally renowned music scene, provides a window onto political, economic and broader social changes. A measure of the profession's vibrancy these days is that in Johannesburg in 2009, leading African fashion magazine, Nigerian-based *Arise*, helped launch a continental African Fashion Week.

RECOMMENDED DESIGNERS AND RESOURCES
Africa

Adama Kai
– Sierra Leone
Alphadi
– Niger
Chichia London
– Tanzania
Farai Simoyi
– Zimbabwe
Gloria Wavamunno
– Uganda
Madam Wokie's Couture
– Sierra Leone
Max Azria
– Tunisia
Mustafa Hassanali
– Tanzania
Evelyn Lambert
– Zimbabwe
Zimbabwe Fashion Week
http://www.
zimbabwefashionweek.com

Left Models wearing faro-faro skirts, a mixture of a vintage denim and lamb leather, by Ivorian designer Etinne Marcel

Model walks the runway at the Arise Magazine African Collection in New York, Fall 2010

Model walks the runway at the Arise Magazine African Collection in New York, Fall 2010

Three Maasai Mara women in traditional clothing

East Africa: Kenya, Ethiopia

East Africa's influences on the global runway are as rich and vital as the textiles for which it is famous.

'80 years ago there was no Paris Fashion Week…We have to take our clothes to a new level.'

Home of the *kanga*, a traditional cotton-printed fabric typical of the region (dubbed the 'African kimono'), East Africa's brightly coloured cottons have cameoed on many a European and American catwalk. The region has also produced a host of dark-skinned, long-legged beauties, including one of modelling's greatest all-time legends, Somalian-born Iman Mohamed Abdulmajid, who has served as muse for prominent designers from Gianni Versace to Donna Karan to Yves Saint Laurent. But in terms of the local fashion scene, as Tanzania's first major fashion designer (and a qualified doctor to boot), Mustafa Hassanali, told the English People's Daily online (www.english.people.com.cn) in 2009, the region still lags behind its continental neighbours to the north, west and south. 'East Africa lags behind West and South African fashion,' he explains. 'But 80 years ago there was no Paris Fashion Week…We have to take our clothes to a new level.'

East Africa's signature garment and the most prominent African textile in Western fashion, the *kanga* (Swahili for 'guinea fowl' on account of its bright colours) was born out of a local African aesthetic coming into contact with European colonial fashions. Balenciaga's Autumn/Winter 2007–08 collection featured mixed-print patchwork dresses with *kanga*-esque fabrics, while Marc Jacobs, for his diffusion line Marc by Marc Jacobs, used the *kanga* as inspiration for prints on breezy, belted sundresses for his Spring/Summer 2010 collection. In the 2010 music video for *Put It in a Love Song*, pop stars Alicia Keys and Beyoncé sport a mash-up of vibrant *kanga*-inspired prints.

Top left Somalian supermodel Iman

Top right Models display Spring/Summer 2011 collection by Suno in New York

Bottom Samburu tribesman in Kenya

Maasai woman in robes with beads, Kenya

Young Samburu woman

Invented by slave women, the *kanga* was inspired by Portuguese traders' *lenços* or handkerchiefs, but, unlike the *lenços*, *kangas* were hand-dyed and brightly printed. Worn as wraps, they are draped and knotted in a variety of ways to form skirts, underarm dresses, tops and head coverings, even doubling up in function as bath towels, dishcloths and mops. By the early 20th century, *kanga* had become an important symbol of freedom as former Zanzibari slaves abandoned the cheaper, undecorated cloths that had signalled both their poverty and their servile status. Around 1910, messages scripted in Swahli began appearing along the edges of the *kanga*. These

messages range from riddles to proverbs such as: *Naogopa simba na meno yake siogopi mtu kwa maneno yake* (I'm afraid of a lion with its strong teeth but not a man with his words) as stated in an article by Daniel Howden published in *The Independent* in 2009.

RECOMMENDED DESIGNERS AND RESOURCES
East Africa

Loin Cloth & Ashes
Tido

Kenya

Of all the East African countries, Kenya, with a booming tourism industry thanks to its world-famous wildlife reserves has had the most influence on the runways of the West (think Christopher Kane's cult must-have gorilla motif from Spring/Summer 2009). For instance, when actress Diane Keaton appeared in the 1977 film *Annie Hall* clutching a Kikuyu (or Kamba) basket as a purse, the bag instantly attained must-have status in the US, becoming known as the 'Kenya bag'. Originally woven by women from sisal fibre in earth tones, bright plastics were incorporated into the mainstream American versions and the style was quickly and widely copied by manufacturers in Korea, the Philippines and Taiwan.

Major designers in Europe and the US also periodically cite the Maasai tribe from Kenya and northern Tanzania – their beadwork, colour palettes and overall style – as inspiration for their creations. Calvin Klein's 1981 runway collection was the first to manifest Maasai influence, and he was followed in 1997, a decade and a half later, by Ralph Lauren, as well as by John Galliano's jewellery for Dior and others. Maasai-influenced collar necklaces turned up in English designer John Rocha's Spring/Summer 2005 line as well as in several Spring/Summer 2007 collections, even working its way into bed linens and home ware collections. In more recent fashion history, Roberto Cavalli, for his second line, Just Cavalli, showed a collection for Spring/Summer 2008 in Milan consisting of brightly colored clashing print patchwork *kanga*-style dresses accessorized with Maasai-beaded necklines. For Spring/Summer 2010, fellow Italian luxury brand Salvatore Ferragamo sent a model down the runway clad in a black gown adorned with concentric circles of beads

Members of the Maasai tribe wearing traditional beaded jewellery

Maasai cultural attire created by the Kenyan Woodgrove College of Design during Kenyan fashion week 2004

Suno Spring/Summer 2011, New York

at the neckline, to the delight of press and buyers, while New York-based Monique L'huillier's collection the same season, with its heavily embellished and sharply constructed pieces, also looked to the beadwork of the Maasai as its baseline reference.

Young and funky New York-based brand SUNO was formed in 2008 by Max Osterweis after more than a decade of collecting textiles on visits to Kenya. Osterweis employs patternmakers in New York and local talent in Kenya for his fair-trade workshop label.

Online UK-based retailer ASOS, as part of their Green Room ethical initiative launched ASOS Africa, which in a similar way to SUNO looks to small Kenyan

cooperatives to source fabrics as well as to produce the clothes, bringing jobs to communities in Kenya and unique fashions to the British high street. 'For Spring/Summer 2010, the focus was on *kangas* and *kitenge* fabrics from the local markets,' explains ASOS's Claire Hamer, who buys the collection for the retailer. 'The Swahili proverbs on the *kangas* were perfect for the bright and colourful season and we wanted to launch with something of heritage from the local communities … Each *kanga* print is only available for approximately two weeks before they move to new designs (East Africa's version of fast fashion!), so it was a challenge to buy for Spring/Summer 2010–[our] team was forever running to and from Mombasa to ensure we got enough for the collection. We have now built stronger relationships with the fabric merchants and we can now have extra *kangas* printed in the same print in order to meet the demand.'

For many Kenyans, of course, despite the success of local textiles and *kangas* abroad, the elite world of high fashion and catwalk couture is either completely unknown or culturally very distant, being such a far cry from their own clothing practices and concerns. The explosion of imported *mitumba* (second-hand clothing) in the 1990s, on the other hand, touched virtually every corner of the nation, bringing a wide array of inexpensive dresses, skirts, trousers, shirts, t-shirts and footwear to many markets, and giving birth to a distinctly Kenyan love of style. A boon for Kenyans on a tight budget, the flood of *mitumba* undercut local textile and clothing industries, challenged designers and blurred some correlations between clothing, wealth and status. Other social and political developments in the 1990s and 2000s also influenced fashion trends in different parts of the country. For example, population movements due to political unrest in neighbouring Somalia brought an influx of middle-class Somalis to Nairobi. Their presence expanded the market for certain types of cloth, a trend that quickly caught on elsewhere.

As far as the local design scene goes, Kenya launched its first fashion week in Nairobi in 2005. Patricia Lulu Mbela, creative force behind the House of Agano, is one of the country's top designers. Inspired by the country's 49 ethnic groups (including, of course, the Maasai), Mbela uses painting, printing, hand-dyeing, marbling and beading, drawing on a regional palette of patterns and motifs to create memorable designs.

RECOMMENDED DESIGNERS AND RESOURCES *Kenya*

Patricia Mbela
(House of Agano)

Models display Spring/Summer 2011 collection by Suno in New York

Hamer woman wearing traditional beading

Matthew Williamson for Pucci Spring/Summer 2008, Milan

Ethiopia

Ethiopian traditional dress rocketed to the forefront of the international fashion scene when British designer Matthew Williamson, aka the 'King of Prints', included two outfits in his Spring/Summer 2008 runway show based on the country's national costume, which the Ethiopian government loudly denounced as copies. The dresses (one a short white tunic with yellow banded detailing, the other a floor-length diamond-print white maxi dress) are near-exact replicas of dresses that are staples in many Ethiopian women's wardrobes. Williamson's cultural copycatting sparked an outrage in Africa's online community, where debates concerning the morality of borrowing a country's national costume, especially when that country is one of the poorest in the world, raged for weeks.

'These are the dresses of our mothers and grandmothers. They symbolise our identity, faith and national pride.'

In an article for Ethiomedia.com, Hewete Haileselassie explains that traditional Ethiopian tailors (*shemanne* in Amharic) earn up to 200 Ethiopian birr a month, the equivalent of £10, while the dress made by the Manchester-born designer, priced at £895, would cost only £30 if created by one of these tailors. A spokeswoman for Matthew Williamson's company said in a statement at the time, 'The design team derived inspiration from various African countries and tribal groups. In presenting his Spring/Summer 2008 collection Matthew Williamson strived to gain recognition and admiration for not only the traditional dress of the Ethiopian people, but also other African communities whose beautiful traditional techniques are also evident in the show.' However, Abdurazak Omer of the Intellectual Property Office in Ethiopia's capital Addis Ababa stated in an interview with the *Telegraph*, 'We are very unhappy with the actions of Matthew Williamson. These are the dresses of our mothers and grandmothers. They symbolise our identity, faith and national pride. Nobody has the right to claim these designs as their own.'

Aside from butting heads with Matthew Williamson, Ethiopia has yet to secure itself a niche on the African fashion radar. Though couture bridal and eveningwear designer Amsale Aberra has found success abroad in the US, where she emigrated in 1973 to study at the Fashion Institute of Technology in New York City. Her company, Amsale, was established in 1986 and specializes in luxury wedding gowns. In addition to her own eponymous boutique on New York's most prestigious shopping street, Madison Avenue, Amsale's bridal designs are stocked at major American luxury retailers such as Bergdorf Goodman, Saks Fifth Avenue and Neiman Marcus. The future of Ethiopian fashion, however, looks promising, as can be seen in the work of young designer Mame Mulatu Debebe, which blends the exotic patterns and fabrics of her native Ethiopia with western contemporary styles. Just as significantly, 2009 saw the birth of the country's first glossy, *Imperia Fashion and Style Magazine*.

RECOMMENDED DESIGNERS AND RESOURCES
Ethiopia

Osman Mohammed
Adila Ismail
Sewasew Hailu
Yamerote Mengis
Mame Mulatu Debebe (MMD)

Matthew Williamson Spring/Summer 2008, London

Model wears a kaftan for Matthew Williamson Spring/Summer 2008, London

Members of the cult of the Sapeur in the Congo

Democratic Republic of Congo, Republic of Congo

Though the Democratic Republic of Congo (formerly Zaire) and Republic of Congo are counted amongst the world's poorest countries, the streets of Kinshasa and Brazzaville, the two respective capitals, heave with a subculture of high fashion set against a backdrop of extreme poverty. While Princess Odette Maniema Krempin may be one of Africa's most famous fashion designers, the Congolese contribution to the fashion world reaches far beyond the traditional culture-inspires-catwalk relationship. Young impoverished urban men, many living in shacks while begging, borrowing and even stealing to fulfil their sartorial dreams of swathing themselves head to toe in Gucci or Armani, have turned high fashion into a demi-religion. At home and in the Diaspora across Belgium and France, they are called the *sapeurs*.

The source of the word *sapeur* is twofold. On the one hand derived from *SAPE*, an acronym for the movement itself, Société des Ambianceurs et Personnes Élégants, the term also happened to double as French slang for a well-dressed person. Now, through the perservering culture of the Congolese dandies, the word has taken on a wholly African meaning. The early roots of *sapeur* culture can be traced to Congolese interactions with European colonialism during the 20th century, specifically to the 1920s and 30s, when privileged Congolese who had spent time in France returned to the country bedecked in dapper suits that were the cutting edge of Paris fashion. Mens' fashion-focused social clubs were established during the 1920s and in the early 1940s and social clubs in the cities of Brazzaville and Kinshasa served as catwalks for wealthy young gentlemen to flaunt their prestigious Western fashions. Then in 1960 both the Democratic Republic of the Congo and the Republic of Congo gained independence (from Belgium and France respectively), and over the next two decades the fashion went from fad to frenzy, becoming a cult unto itself.

Papa Wemba, a blossoming rumba star in the late 1960s, is held to be the father of the movement. He openly spearheaded a fashion revolution, opting for flashy looks over the anti-Western dress code installed by Joseph Mobutu, the first leader of the DRC. Frequent visits to Paris in the early 1980s only stoked Wemba's sartorial fire, and he soon developed a flamboyant, over-the-top signature style that was in direct opposition to Mobutu's sanctioned uniform, a lacklustre Zairian version of the three-piece-suit. Wemba called his elegant new 1930s throwback style 'Ungaru', after French designer Emanuel Ungaro. For Congolese both at home and abroad in the diaspora, the zeitgeist, complete with tapered trousers, brogues, pristinely barbered hair, corncob pipe and tilted fedora, was the picture of irresistible cool.

> *'Let's drop the weapons, let us work and dress elegantly.'*

Paul Smith certainly thought so, as his Spring/Summer 2010 collection was inspired by Daniele Tamagni's photographic tome on the subject of the *Sapeurs*, published in 2009. He immediately crafted his women's collection around Tamagni's colourful and vibrant photos – the opening look, a model clad in a pink suit, orange-striped shirt, red shoes and bowler hat, reproduced in female form the smiling, cigar-smoking *sapeur* winking out from the book's cover. The bright colour palette of the *sapeur* energized the themed menswear collection. Strutting in layered clashes of checks and *ikats*, fabrics made of a technique of weaving that uses resist dye processes and is similar to tie-dye, with bandeaus or bras layered on top, the girls looked like the kind of ladies likely to be found perched on the arm of an Yves Saint Laurent-clad *sapeur* strolling through the streets of Brazzaville. Following on from this success, Smith's next menswear collection went down a similarly *sapeuriste* direction.

Paul Smith walks the runway at the end of his collection Spring/Summer 2010, London

Paul Smith's Spring/Summer 2010 collection inspired by the Congolese Sapeurs

Paul Smith walks the runway at the end of his collection Spring/Summer 2010, London

Today, the *sapeurs'* passion for fashion has morphed into a craze for designer brands. Their mantra is the same as their wealthy female socialite counterparts in the West: the more expensive, the better. The average annual Congolese income is around $100, among the lowest in the world, and Congolese immigrants in Europe are among the poorest, but, while circumstances may oblige them to squat in a shack outside Paris, many still willingly plonk down as much on a jacket at Christian Dior as they would pay for a home in Kinshasa or Brazzaville. In the past, *sapeurs* would spend months saving for a cherished item or even rent or borrow articles of clothing from other, more established *sapeurs*. But today, many young men are not as patient and resort to illegal measures, even abandoning support for their children so as to be able to slide into a new pair of Prada loafers. Congolese shoplifting gangs have sprung up in Brussels and Paris, and even the wealthy Wemba could not support his designer habit forever. He was arrested in 2003 for charging upwards of $4,000 to smuggle Congolese men and women into Europe disguised as members of his band. It doesn't excuse wrongdoing, of course, but what drives these dandy highwaymen into crime is love of fashion and its ability to transform even the most destitute of circumstances into a thing of beauty.

Fashionisto is as fashionisto does and the *sapeurs* are no different, bickering amongst themselves and competing over who's wearing what and whose look cost the most. "It's combat," states Héctor Mediavilla Sabaté in *Colours Magazine* 2004 (www.colorsmagazine.com), a photographer who's been studying the sapeurs since 2003 "and the clothes are the weapons". The Parisian *sapeurs* battle those in Brussels, while Brazzavillians go up against Kinshasans, and so on. 'Fight days' are limited to once every week or so, and the fields of war generally tend to be local outdoor bars.

However, away from the glossy sheen of the fashion battlefield, a *sapeur* by definition is a non-violent individual, despite the violence – three civil wars – that has rocked the Republic of Congo since independence, with activities centred in Brazzaville. They represent an illusion that has been supported by the government, which are trying to normalize a post-war situation. The *SAPE* interrupted its activities when the last civil war started in 1997, and did not reinitiate them until 2002, when their motto became, 'Let's drop the weapons, let us work and dress elegantly.'

RECOMMENDED DESIGNERS AND RESOURCES *Congo*

Princess Odette Maniema Krempin

West Africa: Senegal, Republic of Mali, Ivory Coast, Ghana

For more than a thousand years, West Africa, as one of the world's great producers of cotton, indigo and textiles, has been a sartorial incubator, waiting for the right conditions to blossom. In the 19th century, following on the runaway success of Asian fabrics in European fashion, Western textile manufacturers, particularly the Dutch, looked to West Africa in the hope of setting up factories to replicate the Indonesian wax-dye process but with cheaper production costs. Though this early attempt at outsourcing production flopped as far as the Europeans were concerned (the African-produced textiles failed to ignite the same fervour as the Indonesian originals), locally the cloths sold well on the colonial Gold Coast, and quickly spread to the markets of early 20th-century Nigeria. Soon, the bold coloured and patterned textiles spilled into local fashions and became as ubiquitous throughout West Africa as denim in Europe and the US. West African youths adopted the new fabrics, turning to

Models at Afrik Fashion 2010 in Abidjan, Ivory Coast

Model displays a creation at Afrik Fashion 2010 in Abidjan, Ivory Coast

'In the last ten years there has been a huge rise in emerging fashion designers in West Africa.'

local tailors to rework the cloth around traditional shapes such as women's wrappers and flowing robes, and a West African style aesthetic was born.

Soon the 'African look' enthralled Europe and the long-standing sartorial love affair with the Orient broadened to include a fascination with all things African. At home as well as abroad, a distinctly West African fashion ethos and industry flourished. While Britain controlled The Gambia, Sierra Leone, Ghana and Nigeria throughout the colonial era, France, the epicentre of Western fashion at the time, united Mauritania, Senegal, Guinea, Mali, Burkina Faso, Benin, Ivory Coast and Niger into French West Africa, whose colonial subjects became steeped in the French love of fashion.

As a result, West Africa is home to the most vibrant and thriving fashion markets on the continent. Senegal, Ghana, Ivory Coast and the Republic of Mali have all produced designers who are players on the industry's global main stage. Nigeria, in particular, is home to both an established fashion industry and an emerging local young designer scene, and will be dealt with in more detail in the next chapter. Neighbouring Niger is home to the International Festival of African Fashion, which is held every other year and showcases new local talents alongside international designers such as Yves Saint Laurent, Kenzo, Jean Paul Gaultier and Paco Rabanne.

Thus, West African fashion and West African designers are widely considered to constitute the first generation of the continent's fashion design movement. Led by the Republic of Mali's Chris Seydou, these West Africans were among the group of designers who created the Fédération

Africaine des Créateurs in 1993. The organization has provided a platform for fashion shows and other promotional events aimed at raising the visibility of African design both at home and abroad.

"In the last ten years there has been a huge rise in emerging fashion designers in West Africa," explains celebrity stylist and Ghanaian born UK-based blogger Marian Kihogo. "Before this period, people relied mostly on tailors for made-to-measure commissions. This change in tide paired with the birth of fashion magazines such as *Arise*, *Canoe* and *True Love West Africa* is leading slowly to the formation of a West African fashion industry, as it were. In the present day, designers like Yemi Osunkoya of Kosibah Creations, Adebayo Jones, Deola Sagoe, Fati Asibelua of Momo Fashion, and Aisha Obuobi of Christie Brown are continuing to put this part of Africa on the design map. I can only see it growing stronger and more influential."

West Africa's host of long-legged beauties have also helped draw the eye of the fashion world towards the region. "The late model Katoucha played a big part as a pioneer in the West African fashion scene," explains Kihogo. "The [cause] has also been helped by leading West African models on the international forefront such as Oluchi, Agbani Darego (the first black African Miss World) and Tolula Adeyemi, Salieu Jalloh, Aminata Niaria, Ty Ogunkoya and Kinée Diouf."

RECOMMENDED DESIGNERS AND RESOURCES
West Africa

Telfar

Senegal

Podor-born couturier and cultural activist Oumou Sy is probably Senegal's most successful fashion export, lustrously holding the title of Senegal's Queen of Couture. Like many African designers, Sy has carved out her niche through the reinvention of cloth traditions–fusing African textiles with Western styles as well as integrating newer and

industrial fabrics such as synthetics, jerseys, taffeta and smooth silks into her vivacious creations. Rather than elaborations of a design concept, Sy's works are historical tableaux, raising the arts of cloth, clothing and body adornment to parity with the fine arts, literature and cinema. Her collections have been showcased across Europe, Asia, Africa, and the US.

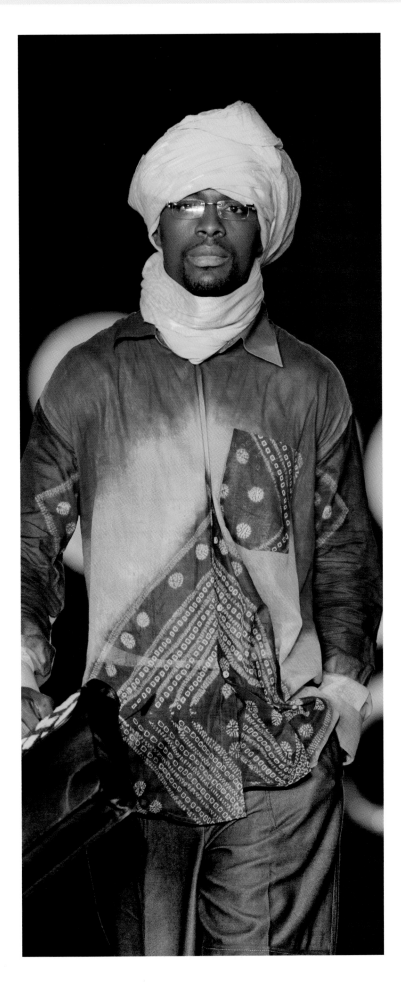

She owns her own eponymous boutiques in Geneva and Paris and has designed for Senegalese singers Baaba Maal and Youssou N'Dour.

Senegal is also home to a host of successful international models. Sadiya Gueye was one of the earliest African models to walk Europe's most prestigious runways. Early in her career, in the 1980s, she caught the eye of Yves Saint Laurent, who promptly adopted her as the muse for his next collection. From there she went on to become one of Paris's premier runway models. Unlike most catwalk sirens, who disappear from the fashion radar once they give up the runway, Sadiye Gueye instead returned to Dakar where she opened a modelling, design and fashion school.

Aminata Niaria, Kinée Diouf and Dji Dieng are the Senegalese beauties currently making waves on the international scene, collectively having walked for designers such as Louis Vuitton, Vivienne Westwood, Fendi and Oscar de la Renta in addition to gracing the pages and covers of the industry's major titles (*Vogue* and *i-D*, to name a couple). Dji Dieng, from Thiès, holds the honour of being the modelling industry's leggiest girl, with an outseam of 125cm (49¼in).

In 2003, Dakar held its first fashion week, presenting a varied assortment of African and Western looks. In recent years, the event has attracted designers from Paris, Cameroon, South Africa, Ivory Coast and Morocco, among others. The organizer of the fashion week since its inception in 2003 has been Adama Ndiaye, a young designer of Sudanese descent, with her own label, Adama Paris.

RECOMMENDED DESIGNERS AND RESOURCES
Senegal

Nafissatou Diop
Oumo Sy
Dakar Fashion Week
http://www.
dakarfashionweek.com

Model displays a creation at Afrik Fashion 2010 in Abidjan, Ivory Coast

Republic of Mali

The Malian fashion scene is one which, primarily influenced by the ethnic tribal groups that make up the country's population (Tuareg, Dogon, Fula Macina, Soninke, Songhai and Bambara), has produced a healthy crop of successful and internationally renowned fashion designers.

Chris Seydou is Mali's, and indeed the entire African continent's, star sartorial success story, as his signature combination of a distinctively Malian textile, *bogolan* (or 'mud cloth'), and European tailoring appealed to both local African women who sought *la mode occidentale* and to Western fashionistas drawn to the exoticism of his designs. The strip-woven cloth is dyed by women using a labour-intensive technique to create bold geometric patterns in white against a deep-brown background. Indigenous Malian girls wear *bogolan* wrappers immediately following their initiations, and hunters wear *bogolan* tunics for protection from wild animals and dangerous spirits. Seydou's earliest use of *bogolan*, in the mid-1970s, was revolutionary because it demonstrated that a textile with deep roots in traditional culture could be transformed into international fashion.

Even Seydou's name itself combines Mali and France, his two primary sources of influence; early in his career, he changed his name from Seydou Doumbia to Chris Seydou in homage to his idol, Christian Dior. He worked and studied in Paris until 1981, when he returned to Africa to establish a studio in Abidjan, Ivory Coast.

Lamine Kouyaté, of the brand Xuly Bet, is a Paris-based Malian designer who first gained recognition in the mid-1990s for his recycled clothing, and now has a stand-alone store in New York's trendy Lower East Side neighbourhood. Using bits gleaned from local flea markets and charity shops, he creates entirely new garments by destroying seams, stitching together random elements of separate garments and often silk-screening slogans and logos onto the resulting shirts, dresses and other garments. Looking to draw attention to the massive influx of second-hand clothing into West Africa and its resulting grip on fashion trends, Kouyaté shies away from concealing the garments' origins, using bright red thread to seam the looks together and leaving old labels in even as he adds his own new ones.

New York-based designer Thakoon Panichgul's Resort 2011 collection, with its eye-popping red and orange prints juxtaposed with neutral tones, pale breezy linens, deconstructed khaki safari jackets and a plastic grocery bag-inspired tote printed with the words 'thank you' seems to gesture towards both Seydou's Senagalese/French ethos and Kouyaté's manifest use of recycling. Thakoon has described his collection as a Parisian going to Africa' and claims 1960s portraits of West African youths by Malian photographer Malick Sidibé as his inspiration.

RECOMMENDED DESIGNERS AND RESOURCES
Republic of Mali

Chris Seydou
Xuly Bet

Opposite Model displays a creation at Afrik Fashion 2010 in Abidjan, Ivory Coast

Model displays a creation at Afrik Fashion 2010 in Abidjan, Ivory Coast

Ivory Coast

Obviously, African influence on fashion extends beyond textiles. Jewellery is another area in which African tribal influence has been paramount, and cascading layers of beads, wooden bangles and other such indigenous accessories have long dominated the international jewellery scene. Franco-Ivorian jewellery designer Michael Kra has done much to bring West African baubles to a position of international acclaim. Having secured his spot on the African fashion scene through his collaborations with leading designers from the region such as Chris Seydou and Alphadi, Michael Kra studied design in the US during the late 1980s and first achieved success in New York with his line of jewellery based on the lost-wax-cast gold-work of the Baule ethnic group of the Ivory Coast and Ghana. From 1991 onwards, his reinterpretations in gold-plated metal were sold under the brand name Reine Pokou, a legendary Baule queen. He has also designed runway jewellery for numerous African shows and has collaborated with Pierre Balmain in Paris.

As for ready-to-wear, Christine King and Patrick Asso are amongst the most successful Ivorian designers. Christine King, born and raised in Abidjan, now based in LA, launched her first womenswear collection in the autumn of 2006, and in 2010 was one of the 16 designers enlisted by Heidi Klum to battle it out on American television for a runway show at Bryant Park on a popular reality show called Project Runway. Her signature look is a layered and textured one that celebrates the arts and crafts of her Ivorian culture, but she also maintains very modern styles and silhouettes.

Patrick Asso, also born in Abidjan, attended a model and fashion school at CARIN'N Couture in Abidjan. Well-known in this and other cities in Africa for creating both mens and womenswear, he showed in Paris in 2008 as well as at *Arise* Africa Fashion Week in Johannesburg in 2009.

RECOMMENDED DESIGNERS AND RESOURCES *Ivory Coast*

Christine King
http://www.christianeking.com
Patrick Asso

Models display creations by Ozwald Boateng, Spring/Summer 2011, London

Ghana

Ozwald Boateng, one of men's fashion's brightest shining beacons, credited with the revival of bespoke tailoring, though born and bred in London, is of Ghanian descent. Born to two Ghanian parents, Ozwald Boateng is widely credited with introducing Savile Row tailoring to a new generation and was the first tailor to stage a runway show in Paris. Though his creations are typically British in their sartorial execution and conceptualization as opposed to Ghanian, consisting of sharp suits in solid colored wools, sleekly fitted jodhpurs, morning and frock coats and so forth, his work does have African elements. The colour combinations and fabric textures he applies to his thoroughly British garment styles have been interpreted as one manifestation of this sensibility—mustard yellow coats teamed with bright green shirts, purple velvet and magenta plaid suits. Even garments in more standard hues

of black, brown and gray have brightly coloured lining. Thus, the "African" in Ozwald Boateng's work boils down to the details.

In 2001, Ozwald Boateng created his first explicitly African collection, entitled "Tribal Traditionalism." Though overtly African-inspired, the collection eschewed the more obvious references to traditional tribal cultures (the reworking of textiles, for instance) and instead embodied the Africa of Boateng's own imagination—urbane, international, neither African nor Western yet adaptable to both worlds. When he was named Creative Director for luxury French Fashion House Givenchy in 2003, he became by far the most visible designer of African descent on the global stage today. As such, when President Barack Obama visited Ghana in 2009, he sought out Ozwald Boateng's tailoring skills to outfit him for the occasion.

Mimi Plange and Aisha Oboubi are two other Ghanian-born designers making headway in the industry. Plange, born in Accra and now based in New York, launched luxury label Boudoir d'Huitres in 2007. Oboubi, still residing and working in Ghana, founded Christie Brown, a luxury women's fashion brand in March 2008, Her clothes are constructed from carefully selected printed African textiles sourced from all over the continent juxtaposed with silks, chiffon denim or jersey. In 2009, Obuobi was awarded the Emerging Designer of the Year Award at the inaugural Arise Africa Fashion Week in Johannesburg.

In 2009, Ghana held its first official fashion event, entitled "Ghana Fashion Weekend." Held in Accra,

the event was organized by the country's largest modelling agency and featured the work of 30 designers. Though the event did not take place the following year, the seeds of a support system for local talent to develop have been sewn.

RECOMMENDED DESIGNERS AND RESOURCES
Ghana

Tina Atiemo
Sika Designs
Jil Couture
Laura Kass

Boudoir D-huitres label (Mimi Plange) http://www.boudoir-dhuitres.com
Christie Brown lavel (Aisha Obuobi)
Ozwald Boateng http://www.ozwaldboateng.co.uk

Ghanaian born designer Mimi Plange at her Boudoir D'huitres Spring/Summer 2011 fashion show, New York

Model in creation by Kofi Ansah at Alta Roma Alta Moda 2009

Nigerian models Mary Jane Unueroh and Fome Emede

Nigeria

Nigeria, with its cohort of emerging young designers and plethora of local fashion publications (one of which has even spawned ongoing runway shows at New York Fashion Week entitled the *African Fashion Collective*), is well on its way to becoming one of the premier fashion capitals of the African continent.

Nigeria's fashion history is closely bound up with its relationship to print media. Since the advent of daily newspapers in the late 1920s, the print media have been an important source of information on fashion and style, especially the *Daily Times of Nigeria* (founded in 1926) and the *West African Pilot* (founded in 1937).

Increased public awareness, via the media, of the importance of national dress and textiles was a part of nationalist politics in the 1950s, in the lead-up to gaining independence from British rule in 1960. The

Nigerian government emulated other West African nations, who had annexed the power of fashion to the cause of independence: nationalists and ordinary citizens alike donned traditional *kente* cloth (a type of silk fabric made of interwoven cloth strips that is native to the Akan people of Ghana and the Ivory Coast) and other indigenous dress as expressions of their national identity.

In the immediate wake of independence Nigeria's first major fashion designer, Shade Thomas (now Thomas-Fahm), stepped into the cultural limelight. Local newspapers and a variety of new Nigerian periodicals popularized her designs in their fashion pages. She was an iconic cultural nationalist and modernized traditional designs by popularizing the use of *aso oke* (Yoruba hand-woven textiles), *adire* (Yoruba hand-dyed fabrics), *akwete* (Igbo hand-woven textiles) and the new made-in-Nigeria cotton prints.

Models walk the runway in pieces by Nigerian designer Bayo Adegbe at 'Fashion for Peace' 2008, Nairobi

Creation by Nigerian designer Bayo Adegbe at 'Fashion for Peace' 2008, Nairobi

In 1986, after another in a long line of military coups overturned a still fragile democracy, the new government instituted the International Monetary Fund's Structural Adjustment Program (SAP) to help pay down the country's crushing international debt. One feature of the SAP budget was a total ban on importing ready-to-wear clothing, new or used. Suddenly, Nigeria's own garment industry flourished, as new customers flocked to local dressmakers and tailors. Established designers in Lagos, many of whom had professional credentials in fashion design, reacted to SAP by 'Nigerianizing' their fashion collections, hoping to create a new Nigerian identity based on a fashion culture that depended on local fabrics.

As a result, in the 1990s a number of fashion houses emerged as trendsetters, Nigeria's new cultural heroes, on a quest to carve out a niche for the country in the fashion industry at large as well as redefining their own sartorial heritage at home. Among the most important were the houses of Labanella, founded by Princess Abah Adesanya; Nikky Africana, founded by Nike Okeowo; and Supreme Stitches (now Rose of Sharon), founded by Folorunso Alakija. The flamboyant acumen of these designers as entrepreneurs, coupled with their natural flair for glamour, quickly catapulted them to celebrity status in the former capital city of Lagos.

As the nineties gave way to the noughties, Nigeria's fashion scene continued to blossom, with a host of up-and-coming young designers, successful fashion publications and, most recently, a burgeoning blogosphere.

Deola Sagoe, from Lagos, is another of this new generation. With designs deeply rooted in African

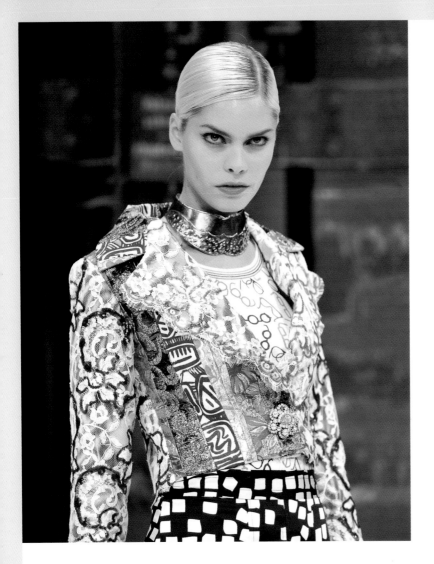

A model wearing a design by Duro Olowu at Charles Vogele Fashion Days 2010, Zurich

Duro Olowu Fall 2007, London

fabrics and aesthetics (such as the use of hand-woven fabrics, extensive use of gold.), Deola Sagoe's collections evoke a genuine African nostalgia. Sagoe has shown collections in the US, Europe and Africa and was the unassuming winner of the African Designs and MNET/Anglo Gold African designs 2000. At *Arise* magazine's African Fashion Collection show at New York Fashion Week in September 2009, Deola Sagoe was one of only three designers showing. Her collection of strong shouldered, body-con minis and embroidered and embellished military jackets and printed leggings was inspired by East African Maasai warriors and 18th-century European military uniforms. She was the only designer who received a standing ovation from the audience.

'In one word Nigerian fashion is "Dynamic".'

Other reputable Nigerian designers at the moment include Ituen Basi, Lisa Folawiyo, Folake Folarin-Coker of Tiffany Amber and the UK-based Emmy Collins.

Abroad, probably Nigeria's best-known fashion figure is London-based designer Duro Olowu. Though only half-African (his father is Nigerian and his mother Jamaican), Nigerian influences run deep in his design aesthetic. First discovered by *Vogue*'s Sally Singer and a buyer from Barneys New York, Olowu is known for stunning fluid dresses rendered in eye-popping prints. For Spring/Summer 2009, Olowu's collection was an African-Parisian mishmash of clashing tribal prints and assorted patterns, for which he has cited as inspiration the 1959 film *Black Orpheus* and the West African masquerade festivals he saw in Nigeria as a child.

Nigeria has also turned out an impressive number of beauties stalking the international runways of Paris, London and New York. Oluchi Onweagba, born in Lagos and now living in New York, won the first ever continent-wide modelling competition, organized by the South African channel M-Net in collaboration with Elite Model Management. She has gone on to grace the covers of Italian *Vogue*, *i-D*, *Elle*, *Untold* and *Surface*, and has also fronted campaigns for Gianfranco Ferré, Gap, Express and Banana Republic. Warebi Martha, also born in Lagos but based in South Africa, has been called the 'Nigeria catwalk queen', and launched her own fashion line in 2009. Francis Nwodu is one of the most popular faces on the mens' side.

In terms of Nigerian fashion media today, *Arise* is probably the most widely recognized African fashion publication in the world, and occupies a unique position among magazines in English-speaking Africa, being the only one that features both pan-African and global content. With a reported circulation of about 60,000 and averaging about 140 pages a month, the magazine is distributed to seven other African countries as well as around Europe and across North America. Its lush and extravagant editorial fashion shoots showcase local designers' work, styled with major European luxury brands and featuring popular black international models like Oluchi Onweagba and Rahma Mohamed.

Arise has on three separate occasions sponsored showcases of African fashion design at New York Fashion Week. In September 2009, the magazine celebrated the launch of its website, AriseLive.com, with a runway show of who's who in the modelling world (Freja Beha Erichsen, Chanel Iman, Iris Strubegger, and Karlie Kloss, to name a few) attended by all major international press. Collections by the Tiffany Amber brand, David Tlale (winner of Johannesburg's equivalent of Project Runway), Eric Raisina and Lisa Folawiyo (her Jewel by Lisa collection) all walked the runway at Bryant Park. Lisa Folawiyo's collection, with its chic, modern interpretation of *kente* prints, stood out in the eyes of the press. *Arise* also co-sponsors African Fashion Week, which was launched in 2009 in Johannesburg.

"Nigerian fashion is in its growth stages and still evolving," explains Terence Sambo, the Lagos-born and bred blogger behind the popular site OneNigerianBoy.blogspot.com. "It is certainly colourful and its deep Afro roots can be traced to its fabrication (mostly African print), yet Nigerian design still follows global trends. In one word Nigerian fashion is 'Dynamic'."

RECOMMENDED DESIGNERS AND RESOURCES *Nigeria*

Toju Fojeh
Tsemaye Binitie
Viv La Resistance
Tiffany Amber
Zed Eye
Adebayo Jones
Aimas
Autumn Adeigbo
Bridget Awosika
Buki Akib
Duro Olowu
Ejiro Amos-Tafiri
House of Farrah
House of Nwocha
House of Versatile Style
Jewel by Lisa
Kareema Mak
Kemkemstudio
Kiki Kamanu
Odio Mimonet
Okunoren Twins
Peridot & Ruby
Phunk Afrique
Qetura
Samantha Cole
Lanre Da Silva
Lola Faturoti
MOMO
Bunmi Koko
http://www.bunmikoko.com
Deola Sagoe
http://www.deolasagoe.net
Ituen Basi
http://www.ituenbasi.com

Left A model wearing a design by Duro Olowu at Charles Vogele Fashion Days 2010, Zurich

South Africa

South Africa is a country of many cultural layers and eleven official languages, where memories of nearly half a century of apartheid still linger in the public consciousness. Yet this diversity of cultures coupled with such a turbulent political history has fostered a complex and intriguing recent history of dress: fashion statements in South Africa are often also political ones. Nelson Mandela, South Africa's first post-apartheid president and popularizer of the Madiba shirt, is not only the nation's most famous leader, but also its most famous fashion icon. "Of course clothes are political," said South African couturier Amanda Laird Cherry was quoted in the *Berg Fashion Library*

> ## 'Of course clothes are political.'

(p. 152) in 2006. "'If you understand the innuendos of fabric and cut, or even the way a belt is worn, then you'll notice them, and you'll understand their connection to the history of this country.'"

The ruling National Party government during the apartheid years (1948–94) drew its mandate from the minority white population, principally the Afrikaners, as, among other basic human rights violations, the indigenous black population was denied the right to vote. The government further exploited differences among the country's various ethnicities. Tribes were divided into separate 'nations' and denied South African citizenship. Operating along the lines of divide and conquer,

Opposite Tatum Keshwar, Miss South Africa 2009, in Stoned Cherrie at Cape Town Fashion Week 2010
Top Thousands of Zulu maidens gather for annual Reed Dance

Nelson Mandela wearing Madiba shirt in 2008

South African woman wearing Xhosa beaded ewellery

white politicians cynically homed in on the country's vast array of traditional ethnic dress as a means of emphasizing the differences between local tribal groups. Zulu ear plugs, women's *isicholo* headdresses and the animal-skin regalia of chiefs became clichés of Zulu ethnicity. Similarly, the Ndebele tribe, who pile silver-coloured bangles on their necks, wrists and ankles, and wear colour-blocked blankets of red, blue, yellow and purple, were singled out for their picturesque and primitive 'otherness', while turbaned, pipe-smoking women in red blankets crystallized into stereotypes of the Xhosa people. Soon, the persistent wearing of ethnic dress in urban centres came to symbolize a form of resistance to the invading colonial ideologies.

Because dress was such a visible way of making a statement, its images and stereotypes were splashed across the global media in 1994, as the world watched the apartheid regime come to an end. In the years since then these tribal identities have individually entered the public imagination, inserting themselves into the minds of fashion designers and showing up on some of the world's glossiest catwalks. In Spring 2005 for instance, designer Daryl Kerrigan of the label Daryl K showed a collection of hand-painted slouchy cotton separates and bold patterns rendered in soft tones which she dubbed 'Zulu cowboy'. Alexandre Herchcovitch, for Spring/Summer 2007, was inspired by the Ndebele tribe and their legendary beadwork. He introduced a print infused with an Ndebelian-style geometry, which upon closer inspection revealed itself to be constructed of tessellated razor blades instead of traditional motifs. Sophie Buhai and Lisa Mayock, the design duo behind New York-based label Vena Cava, looked beyond the Ndebele's famous accessories to the tribe's bright, graphic wall murals as inspiration for their Spring/Summer 2010 collection.

The close connection between fashion and politics was highlighted dramatically in 1962 when Nelson Mandela, on trial for attempting to overthrow the government, bucked the legal dress code and appeared in court on the day of his sentencing wearing the traditional dress of his royal Thembu lineage. Mandela's sartorial stunt sparked a lively debate in the press about whether or not African leaders should wear 'tribal' dress, because this could be seen as playing directly into the hands of their white oppressors. But, ever the style chameleon, in 1994, when Mandela was installed as president, he wore an elegant tailored suit of international style – a sign of both his statesmanship and his determination to build a nation that was not divided along racial or ethnic lines. In the course of his presidency, he adopted what has become known as the Madiba shirt, based on a patterned Indonesian-style silk shirt that he had once received as a gift, designed by Desré Buirski. This shirt has become his signature, and has been worn by every major world leader who has ventured to South Africa on state affairs or had the honour to receive its president. Named after his honorary tribal title, over the years Mandela has donned a vast array of Madibas in varying colours, fabrics and prints on both formal and informal occasions. The late Italian designer Gianni Versace once created a Madiba shirt, which his sister

Donatella donated to a charity auction in honour of the great peacekeeping leader, an event called Versace for Africa, headed by Naomi Campbell, which took place in 2009. Ever a friend of the fashion industry, Mandela himself graced the cover of *Esquire* Spain in May 2010, while his 90th birthday bash, in 2008, was packed with the most A-list of the A-list – including Robert DeNiro, Denzel Washington and even Oprah Winfrey. The 'Mandela look' has come to symbolize a sort of compromise between the West and Africa, as well as reflecting a new emerging South African fashion scene, taking its first tentative steps in a country seeking to define itself anew under black majority rule.

In using dress to help create a post-apartheid identity, South Africans have not only expressed pride in their South African-ness but have also used fashion to express a new sense of being connected to the larger continent by infusing their Western wardrobes with a decidedly African flair. The Victorian-inspired dress and colourful headwraps of South Africa's Xhosa

Zulu women clad in traditional dress during a street parade carnival

Stoned Cherrie
South African
Fashion Show

Model walks the runway in a bright pink dress by South African label, Stoned Cherrie

A model wears Lalesso during Cape Town fashion week 2008

peoples, developed following 19th-century contact with European settlers, became, and remain to this day, particularly popular among women expressing their ethnic pride and South African identity. Semi-flared skirts from the same ethnic origin, based on a Victorian pattern, were Africanized with braiding, stitching and buttons, and eventually transformed for the catwalk by the iconic South African brand Sun Goddess. Other innovative responses to ethnic traditions and vintage styles have found their way into fashion collections, where modern interpretations of Dutch or English settler styles intermingle with re-imagined ethnic dress and Indian saris made of African-print fabric. Accordingly, the inspirations and innovations on the catwalks of Johannesburg and Cape Town are as diverse as South Africa itself.

The brand Lalesso, launched in 2005 by Olivia Kennaway and Alice Heusser, looks to the attire of local women in Africa's coastal regions for inspiration, where the traditional attire is the *kanga* (also known as *lesso*), with its intrinsic patterns and punchy colours. An exclusively summer fashion and lifestyle brand, Lalesso brings the vibrancy of Africa in a ready-to-wear package and has been featured in *Vogue*, *Cosmopolitan*, *Elle*, *Marie Claire* and *Glamour*. The duo have shown at Africa Fashion Week (launched in 2009) and Durban Fashion Week, and opened Cape Town Fashion Week 2008. Celebrities including Kate Moss and Rihanna have worn the label, which is the only South African brand with a concession in British high-street retail staple Topshop.

The brand Strangelove uses performance and sculptural garments to comment on their country's history. Another brand, Stoned Cherrie, is best known for its influential 'Sophiatown' styles, named for a community outside Johannesburg where urban black culture flourished in the 1940s and '50s before, beginning in the mid-1950s, the population was forcibly removed by the apartheid government, its buildings razed. The culture of Sophiatown was international and looked just as much to Harlem as Johannesburg. Stoned Cherrie's Sophiatown-inspired clothing includes 1940s style dresses and hats, worn with T-shirts emblazoned with old covers from *Drum Magazine*, a key chronicler of township life in the early years of apartheid.

South African fashion today embodies an ongoing conversation with the rest of Africa and the world beyond. Major American brands infiltrate the market as they do everywhere, but remain a symbol of wealth for a small urban elite. Economic and class differences still loom large in the country, but this same poverty and challenging political history has led to fashion innovation on both the catwalks and the streets. In terms of street style, clever South African teens resourcefully restyling a second-hand garment have provided an inspiration to designers both in Africa and abroad.

A model wears Lalesso during Cape Town fashion week 2008

RECOMMENDED DESIGNERS AND RESOURCES
South Africa

Abigail Betz
Abigail Keats
Clive Rundle
Colleen Eitzen
Craig Jacobs
David Tlale
Spero Villioti
Stoned Cherrie
Sun Goddess
Suzaan Heyns
Tanya Demby
Thula Sindi
Phumzile Langa
RjKay
Amanda Laird Cherry
Diamond Face Couture
African Mosaiques
Nadine Holloway
Marianne Fassler
Lunar
Machere
Errol Arendz
Guillotine
Gavin Rajah
Kluk CGDT
Lalesso
Albertus Swanepoel
Johannesburg Fashion Week
http://www.jfw2011.co.za

Yves Saint Laurent
model during the
World Cup Final
in France, 1998

Model wears a fez for Yves Saint Lauren Spring/Summer 2011, Paris

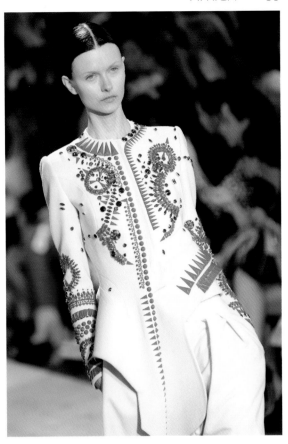

Givenchy Haute Couture, Fall 2010. Paris

Morocco

Moroccan influence has long captured the imagination of fashion designers in the West. Many of the Spring/Summer and resort-season wardrobe staples issue from a Moroccan aesthetic, be it shapes such as the kaftan and *djellaba* or intricate ornamentation and embroidery. Without the influence of traditional Moroccan dress, summer styles today (and beachwear, in particular) would be a lot less colourful and certainly a lot less chic.

Though born in neighbouring Algeria, Yves Saint Laurent always maintained a second home amongst the rich hippies of Marrakesh and took refuge there during the Paris anarchy of May 1968, returning with the sketches for a collection that, although modelled in the old, staid mannequin manner, was described as the 'first post-couture'. His 1977 and 1978 shows were also magnificent pageants referencing exotic pasts, including that of Morocco. When the designer died in 2008, his body was cremated and ashes were scattered in Marrakesh in the Majorelle Garden, a

botanical garden he and his partner Pierre Bergé had bought in 1980 and restored.

For his menswear Spring 2011 show, the brand's Creative Director Stefano Pilati went back to the house's founder's love of North Africa, as signified by the presence of voluminous layered coats, fringed detailing and even the odd fez capping the heads of a few of the models. Stefano Pilati claimed that he was inspired in particular by the influence of American expatriate writer and composer Paul Bowles, a dapper gentleman who spent many years translating Moroccan folklore and composing music, and whose wife, fellow writer Jane, was known for her exceedingly boyish look whilst living in Tangier. In this collection's take on his house's founder's love affair with Marrakech amounted a somber color palette, jackets with their sides slit to resemble djellaba, sandals for footwear, and a fez or two perched atop the models' heads.

Ralph Lauren Spring/Summer 2009, New York

Ralph Lauren Spring/Summer 2009, New York

In recent fashion history, Ralph Lauren for Spring/Summer 2009 utterly enchanted by the splendour of Moroccan garments, showed a collection entirely inspired by the seductive mystique and glamour of the country, including low-slung gold beaded harem trousers and a silk-linen gauze strapless gown in neutral hues.

Throughout history the presence of the Sahara Desert has made for distinct cultural differences between northern Africa and the rest of Africa. Thus the seafaring civilizations of the Phoenicians, Greeks, Romans and others facilitated communication and migration across the Mediterranean, and the cultures of North Africa became much more closely tied to southwestern Asia and Europe than to Sub-Saharan Africa.

When the Phoenicians and later the Romans first settled in Morocco, they encountered the indigenous

peoples of North Africa west of the Nile Valley, including the Berber, who still make up about half of the Moroccan population today. Then in the 7th century Arabs moved into Morocco, founding the city of Fez and gradually converting the Berbers to Islam. To this day, Berber and Arab cultures remain the dominant cultural forces in the country and continue to excite and inspire foreigners. Designer Riccardo Tisci of French couture house Givenchy, for for the house's Autumn/Winter 2009 couture collection, looked to the ethnography of the Berber people for inspiration for his collection of strongly tailored *sarouel*-influenced, trousers, hoods, and veiled and draped silhouettes covered with Middle Eastern-style gold embroidery.

The art form of embroidery on silk, cotton and linen so famously associated with Morocco evolved centuries ago from an elaborate tradition of women decorating their hands and feet with

Givenchy
Haute Couture,
Fall 2010, Paris

Collection of Moroccan jewellery

henna, which is cultivated in the southern parts of the country. At some point, the designs crept off the women's skin and onto their shawls, handkerchiefs and headscarves. Soon, these intricate embroideries decorated almost every aspect of domestic interior spaces, from cushions and curtains to tablecloths and mats. Traditionally, a Moroccan girl's dowry, a set of richly embroidered curtains, bed covers and tablecloths, among other bits, could easily take a lifetime for her female forebears to complete.

'At Missoni the kaftan has always been a staple piece.'

Cities such as Tétouan, Chaouen, Meknès, Rabat, Salé, Azemmour and Fez are all known for their unique embroidery styles, techniques, colours and fabrics. Fez embroidery is the most famous, its highly graphic and geometric design making it easy to identify. The triangle motif represents the eye, but may also symbolize the female sex if there are other triangles in each corner. The hand of Fatima is also embroidered for protection against the evil eye. Unfortunately today, relatively few Moroccan women practice the art of hand embroidery and most items are now made by machines.

Spanish-born New York-based designer Carolina Herrera featured rich Moroccan embroideries in her Spring/Summer 2000 range of sophisticated pieces adorned in pink and chartreuse beads. And Miuccia Prada's Spring/Summer 2002 collection for Miu Miu was riddled with heavily Moroccan-influenced embroidery adorning an A-line skirt's hemline here or a tailored jacket there, serving as a unifying motif for the entire collection. Indian-born designer Naeem Khan, for Spring/Summer 2008, showed a collection of luxe and brightly coloured paisley-embroidered floor-length kaftans, which, in their bohemian elegance, referenced Dutch actress Talitha Getty, the supposed pioneer of 'Moroccan heiress chic' in the late 1960s.

The *djellaba*, a long, loose-fitting outer robe with full sleeves and a hood, is the traditional dress of Moroccan men, and is also worn throughout North Africa and Arabic-speaking countries across the

Matthew Williamson Spring/Summer 2009, New York

Emilio Pucci Spring/Summer 2010, Milan

Mediterranean. Parisian designer Anne Valérie Hash, for her Autumn/Winter 2002 couture collection, drew upon Moroccan menswear in general and elements of the *djellaba* in particular. She reworked Western suiting fabrics to make baggy, ethnic trousers. Dress shirts took on various incarnations of the *djellaba* and in a gender reversal, an oversized Moroccan men's shirt became a skirt, with the collar at the waist and the arms tied around the back.

All these influences, however, pale in comparison to the influence of Morocco's most famous garment, which the country's most important fashion event even takes as its *nom de théâtre*. Launched in 1996 by the magazine *Femmes du Maroc* CAFTAN is the single most important event of Moroccan and Arabic haute couture. Each edition is devoted to the development of Moroccan and Eastern kaftan haute couture, and designers are encouraged to link the past to the present through innovation to ensure that the kaftan, while continuing to evolve in a modern world, retains its traditional essence.

The kaftan's value to contemporary fashion is certainly indubitable. On account of its versatility (it fits any body shape and options abound for every budget) since around the 1960s, breezy, brightly printed kaftans have been the go-to staple for the stylish woman lounging around the pool– the Riviera would not have been the same without it. But in recent years, it has been reworked in luxurious, flowing, embellished silks to function on the runway as eveningwear, or even as short, youthful minis. The kaftan has officially transitioned from holiday favourite to year-round wardrobe staple, appearing in prestigious collections by the likes of Diane Von Fürstenburg, Anna Sui, Elie Saab, Dior Homme, Blumarine, Missoni, Jean Paul Gaultier, Matthew Williamson, Armani and Emilio Pucci. "At Missoni the kaftan has always been a staple piece," Angela Missoni, Creative Director of her family's eponymous brand, which is known for its beachwear, once told the *Financial Times*. "For me, the appeal lies in the versatility and laid-back glamour for the wearer, taking you seamlessly from the poolside or beach to a restaurant or bar at night."

Moroccan fashion today, with events such as CAFTAN, seeks proudly to preserve its traditional styles whilst still modernizing for a Westernized and globalized market. The country's princess, Lalla Salma, wife of the current king, Mohammed VI, is its style icon. Generally clad head to toe in Chanel, Dior, Gucci or Prada, the Princess Consort also wears traditional and locally produced Moroccan garments, including kaftans, and has earned herself the tile of the African continent's 'First Lady of Style'.

In the 1980s, young female Moroccan designers such as Tamy Tazi and Fadilah Berrada began to experiment with traditional dress and combine it with their training in Western fashion. Tazi, for example, replaced the voluminous shape of the kaftan, which was designed to hide a woman's body, for one that emphasizes the female form, and she also revived interest in centuries-old embroidery and

the bell-shaped sleeves of the past. Some designers, such as Noureddine Amir, reject imported fabrics and only work with local materials. Over the years, these designers have established a Moroccan haute-couture culture that caters to a specific Moroccan elite. By the mid-1990s, there was an increasing focus on the haute-couture kaftan through new women's fashion magazines such as *Femmes du Maroc*. First published in 1995, this glossy is the most widely read French-language monthly magazine in the country, and has an Arabic sister publication, *Nissae Min Al Maghreb*, launched in 2000.

Morocco's most famous fashion export, without question, is Paris-based, pop-culture-obsessed avant-garde designer Jean-Charles de Castelbajac. The Casablanca-born fashion star of the 1970's and 1980s has carved out a cult niche for himself with his brightly coloured, often sequined, iconically

Princess Lalla Salma of Morocco

Model wearing harem trousers for Givenchy Haute Couture Fall 2010, Paris

Brightly coloured *Babouches* (Moroccan slippers) on sale in Marrakech

pop-culture-inspired creations. The mid-1970s saw him dress actress Farah Fawcett for hit TV series *Charlie's Angels* and collaborating with musicians Mick Jagger and Elton John. Megastar Madonna and supermodel Helena Christensen at different times have both donned one of his teddy-bear dresses, and his rainbow-flag vestments once graced the body of Pope John Paul II. In 2006, London's Victoria and Albert Museum curated a major retrospective of his fascinatingly colourful 45-year career.

Like Jean-Charles de Castelbajac, most of Morocco's fashion talents choose to set up their ateliers beyond the walls of Casablanca. Menswear designer Hisham Oumlil, best-known for his pristine suiting and an original take on the trench coat, is based in New York, where he has shown seven collections. Aziz Bekkaoui, an artist and fashion designer born in Berkane, is now based in Amsterdam. After graduating from the Fashion Department at Arnhem Art Academy in 1995, he came to prominence the following year when he won the Grand Prix for best women's wear at France's Festival International des Arts de la Mode for his daring, playful designs. He has since shown in Amsterdam, London, Austria and France.

Finally, Samira Haddouchi is a young Moroccan designer famous for the kaftan she designed for Lebanese singer Haifa Wehbe, which appeared on the cover of numerous women's magazines and newspapers, and which Hollywood actress Susan Sarandon also wore at the 6th Marrakesh International Film Festival.

From Casablanca to Marrakech, the desert charms of Morocco have always and will always continue to romance and inspire designers at home and abroad. From the departed icon Yves Saint Laurent, whose love for the place was so great, his ashes were spread there instead of his native Algeria, to Jean-Charles de Castelbajac showing his playful collections on the runways of Paris, to the launch of the local event CAFTAN, it seems that it seems that fashion's love affair with Morocco, is as classic and enduring as the film Casablanca itself.

RECOMMENDED DESIGNERS AND RESOURCES
Morocco

Hisham Oumlil
Aziz Bekkaoui
http://www.aziz.nl
Jean-Charles de Castelbajac
Samira Haddouchi
Alber Elbaz for Lanvin
Amine Bendriouich

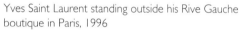

Yves Saint Laurent standing outside his Rive Gauche boutique in Paris, 1996

Model displays leopard print kaftan for Yves Saint Laurent Spring/Summer 2002, Paris

Algeria

Algeria's claim to fashion fame boils down to the success of one legendary figure: Yves Saint Laurent. Paris's king of couture, the man who single-handedly popularized ready-to-wear fashion in the 1960s, whose titan of a fashion house spawned fashion permatrends from the safari look to the androgynous Weimar (or Le Smoking) tuxedos and even the jumpsuit, was in fact North African.

Born in French-ruled Algeria in 1936, Yves Saint Laurent is considered one of the most influential and celebrated designers in modern fashion history. His mark on succeeding generations of would-be catwalk kings is as inextricable from their designer DNA as the colour black from the fashion palette. In 1953, at the age of just 17, the young Yves Saint Laurent submitted three sketches to a contest for young fashion designers, organized by the International Wool Secretariat. He came third and was invited to attend the awards ceremony in Paris later that year.

Over the course of his career, despite ascending to the height of Parisian fashion royalty and heading up the House of Christian Dior at the tender age of 21 after Dior's sudden early death, Yves Saint Laurent never forgot his Algerian roots in his fashions. He was famously inspired by the bright colours and vibrant prints of the North Africa of his childhood. For Spring/Summer 1967, his collection was inspired by African art and is known as the African collection. Models slinked down the runway in African-print fabrics in natural hues and embellished with bits of wood, copper bangles, glass beads and ample helpings of raffia. The following year saw Yves Saint Laurent explore the other side of the African experience, casting the sartorial spotlight on the colonizers rather than the colonized, with the introduction of the safari look.

Since before the birth of Christ, the territory and peoples of Algeria have been ruled by one or another power from across the Mediterranean: Rome, Spain,

'This fashion show is an opportunity for young Algerians to discover haute-couture fashion. It's a mix between the beauty of Algeria and haute couture.'

Turkey and latterly France. These influences combined with the long-standing presence of Islam and the culture of the native Berber tribes have made the country a cultural melting pot, especially where dress is concerned. In Algiers, the country's capital and most cosmopolitan city, fashion trends and materials have always changed as traders came and went, streaming in from Morocco in the west, Libya in the east and from across the Mediterranean. However, several mainstays of Algerian traditional dress have remained characteristic over many years: a *caraco*, or embroidered-silk short jacket; a *ghila*, of similar shape and material, namely velvet, sporting a low oval décolleté; the embroidered flat *chechia*; and an open kaftan. The region west of Algiers – in the past centered on the ancient cities of Tlemcen and Mascara, and since the 19th century, on Oran, birthplace of Saint Laurent – is culturally close to Morocco, which explains the designer's affinity for the garb of Algeria's neighbour.

The French, who invaded and captured Algiers in 1830 and held colonial power until 1962, were fascinated by local Algerian fashion and aimed to preserve it and adapt it to their own use, at least in the political sphere. In the mid-19th century, coincidental with the opening of Asia to the West and the influx of Eastern artefacts into the hands of Western collectors and museums, Paris fell under the spell of 'oriental' fashion and looked to its African colonies to fuel the fascination. As if to capture a romanticism that had disappeared with the French Revolution, oriental dress was worn by many artists and even dignitaries at Napoleon III's court. Algeria allowed French romantics, army officers and, to a lesser degree, civilians to indulge in heroic splendour and the display of social hierarchies that had disappeared at home.

Since gaining independence in 1962, the Algerian Government has made a push to kick start industrial development by looking to produce European-style clothing. Women who had gained partial access to the public sphere dressed in similar ways to their French counterparts, though most women either maintained a more traditional style or developed a compromise between styles–sometimes also

Yves Saint Laurent walks the catwalk at the end of his Haute Couture Spring/Summer 2000 collection, Paris

Model wears black corseted damask silk dress with red wildflower print for Yves Saint Laurent Fall 1995, Paris

Yves Saint Laurent High Fashion Show Fall 1989, Paris

Algerian woman in traditional dress c.1910

inspired by Egyptian influence, as seen on television. Traditional dress became increasingly associated with the house or was reserved for special occasions. In the 1980s, women adopted the *hijab* with either a long simple robe or jeans, a style that saw Algerian fashion once more make its mark in France as second-generation immigrants from North Africa started to wear the same outfit in French suburbs. This has incurred the displeasure of the French Government, which in 2010 passed a law banning the wearing of the *hijab* in public places.

Several young designers, such as Nassila, Yasmina, Akli Boudarene and many others, have recently made names for themselves by adapting traditional regional dress to new materials and modified styles. *Dzeriet* is a French-language lifestyle glossy magazine first published in 2004, with extensive features on fashion and a readership of 2 million every month. On 6th November 2008, the magazine organized a fashion show in Algiers. The show displayed the Autumn/Winter 2008 women's haute couture collection by Mexican designer Jorge Castellanos, who was showing in Algeria for the first time. All of the models were Algerian. *Dzeriet's* Editor, Mr

Naim, stated in a press release, 'This fashion show is an opportunity for young Algerians to discover haute-couture fashion. It's a mix between the beauty of Algeria and haute couture.'

These designers have thus furthered national homogeneity and led a cultural revival of Algerian heritage among second-generation immigrants in France. Indeed, most designers run shops and fashion shows in both Algeria and France, and numerous French websites with a large second-generation immigrant audience promote and discuss their products. Because so many of these designers work in both Algeria and France, the boundaries between French and Algerian design are not always easy to see. Indeed, North African fashion has found many admirers among young French women.

RECOMMENDED DESIGNERS AND RESOURCES
Algeria

Yves Saint Laurent
Nassila
Yasmina
Akli Boudarene

Elizabeth Taylor as Cleopatra, 1963

Tutankhamun

Egypt

No ancient civilization has captured and coloured man's imagination quite like that of Egypt's mighty Pharaohs. Arguably the birthplace of luxury as we know it (ancient Egyptians wore the finest jewellery, perfumed themselves with almond, jasmine, myrrh and roses), the Nile Valley and all its treasures, both real and imaginary, excavated and still buried deep, has been a never-ending font of inspiration for fashion designers ever since British archaeologist Howard Carter first cracked open the tomb of King Tutankhamun, revealing the splendour of ancient Egypt to a mesmerized world. In recent years, Egypt has touched the haute couture collections of John Galliano for Christian Dior from Spring/Summer 2004 (with its spectacular gold headdresses, sphinx masks and even tunics of crocodile leather), and Alexander McQueen in his infamous witchcraft collection from Autumn/Winter 2007 (which saw models with Nefertiti hairdos and one girl clad in a metallic lycra bodysuit styled to look like a figure come to life from inside a sarcophagus). You need

only utter the name Cleopatra to evoke a striking image of a powerful fashion icon. Elizabeth Taylor *circa* 1963, her head fully adorned in a gold-beaded headdress (mimicking the wigs of human hair worn by both men and women in the Pharaonic period to stay cool and prevent lice), her curvaceous body swathed in equally brilliant beaded body-hugging evening columns, snake décolletage coiled at the ready, has served as muse for countless designers since. In fashion, a nod to Egypt signifies a love of luxury and the decadence of it all.

The history of dress in Egypt is long and complicated and highly influenced by the country's geographical location at the crossroads of Asia, Africa and Europe. The triangular loincloth for both him and her was the go-to garment from the time of the Old Kingdom (2686–2181BC) onward. The other important unisex article of clothing was the tunic, introduced into Egypt around 1600BC. A rectangle of cloth folded in half and sewn down the sides, the tunic leaves holes at the top for the arms with a slit for the head. Women normally wore floor-length tunics, while men wore knee to ankle-length. The more important the person, the longer and wider the tunic. Tunics donned by a pharaoh were often highly decorated in a variety of techniques, such as multicoloured tapestry weave, embroidery, beading and gold appliqué.

> '*I looked at ancient Egyptian costume, and there's something Sixties in there you see in a lot of movies on Greek television.*'

Long before Diane von Fürstenberg introduced her jersey wraparound dresses, women in ancient Egypt wrapped lengths of linen around their bodies in a number of ways with the so-called sheath dress. More elaborate sheath dresses were knotted at the shoulder and during the Old Kingdom some women wore tight-fitting, long-sleeved dresses decorated with horizontal pleats. Wraparound dresses gradually became elaborate creations that were wrapped, draped, tucked and knotted in complex and elegant ways, and were often worn over a tunic, giving a wider range of expressive dress and driving a cultural awareness of

fashion. In the iconic manner of Elizabeth Taylor's 1963 fashion statement, another type of sheath was made from beads. Some dresses were beaded directly, while others were made of a net of beads that was placed over the rap, a technique still used by designers today.

Egyptians have worn jewellery since prehistoric times. Until the Greco-Roman period, men and women wore head and hair decorations, earrings and ear studs, and many types of necklaces, armbands, bracelets, rings and anklets. The trinkets were often decorated with intricate designs based on characters and events from mythology and have survived alongside their embalmed wearers to influence legions of jewellers and accessories designers alike. Roberto Cavalli, for Autumn/Winter 2007 showed a collection infused with Egyptian-inspired accessories: ivory necklaces and furs layered in tiers interspersed with sparkling crystals. John Galliano, repeatedly inspired by ancient Egypt, having again plundered the Nile Valley for his Spring/Summer 2009 ready-to-wear collection, the following season topped off his models with Egyptian-style crowns and diadems. Greek designer Sophia Kolosalaki, for

Roberto Cavalli Autumn/Winter 2007, Milan

Roberto Cavalli Autumn/Winter 2007, Milan

Egyptian mummy inspired creation at Alexander McQueen Autumn/Winter 2007, Paris

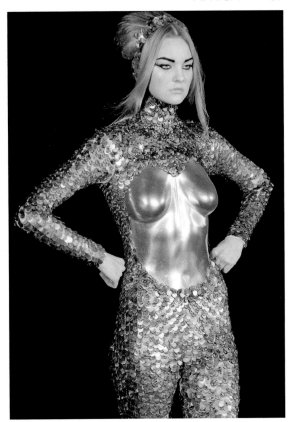

Alexander McQueen Autumn/Winter 2007, Paris

Spring/Summer 2009, accessorized her collection of python bodices and chiffons printed with hieroglyphic-like patterns, with massive snake-embossed gold cuffs and dangling animal-motif earrings. 'I looked at ancient Egyptian costume, and there's something Sixties in there you see in a lot of movies on Greek television,' she told Style.com after the show. 'But, you know, it's always done in a young and ironic way.'

Cosmetics were worn from the prehistoric period onward and women in Egypt today still outline their eyes with kohl (black eyeliner). Eye paint was the most common cosmetic and was used to shield the eyes from the sun. Eye paints were made of green copper oxide (malachite) and black lead galena. Lipstick and a form of rouge were also occasionally used.

The Greco-Roman period dates from about 332BC to 645AD and is normally divided into the Ptolemaic, Roman and Byzantine periods, after which Egypt was absorbed into the new Islamic Empire. Mummy portraits fashionable in the early Roman period provide abundant sources of information on the Romanized elite of the time. Greeks and Romans introduced new loom technologies, allowing a

wider range of weaves including twills, tapestry, compound weaves, damasks and brocades. As a result, clothing in the Roman era is much more colourful and varied than the garments worn during previous periods. This early junction of West and East was immortalized, of course, by the romance of Ptolemaic Queen Cleopatra VII and the Roman Marc Antony in the 1st century AD. Despite Egypt's status as a subject kingdom within the Roman Empire, Roman fashions were not slavishly adopted but rather reinterpreted to fit the Egyptian context. For example, a colourful Roman tunic could be worn underneath a Pharaonic wraparound dress.

Around 645 AD Egypt became part of the rapidly spreading Islamic Empire, which eventually stretched from Spain to Central Asia. The attire of the early Muslim court was influenced by Arab as well as Persian and Byzantine fashions. The arrival of the Turkish Ottomans in 1517 had a considerable impact on dress in urban centres such as Cairo and Alexandria. Ottoman Turks and Egyptians employed by them, as well as those wishing to emulate the new social elite, wore Ottoman dress. Ottoman attire continued well into the 19th century and changed according to the fashions of the court at Istanbul.

Model wearing creation by Greek-born British designer
Sophia Kokosalaki Spring/Summer 2009, Paris

Model wearing creation by Greek-born British designer
Sophia Kokosalaki Spring/Summer 2009, Paris

However, with the end of the Ottoman Empire (officially in 1918), Turkish-style garments virtually vanished from the Egyptian sartorial repertoire.

'People are finally seeing the importance of looking nice and dressing up and now they are starting to really have access.'

When the tomb of King Tutankhamun was discovered in 1922, a craze for Egyptian artefacts ensued, known as 'Egyptomania'. The craze touched all walks of popular culture, from cinema, fashion and jewellery to architecture, particularly the Art Deco style of design, whose familiar angular forms and geometric patterns draw heavily upon ancient Egyptian imagery. Jewellers such as Cartier and Boucheron were quick to jump on board, as Egyptian influence encouraged the use of stones such as lapis lazuli, coral, jade and onyx as well as a plethora of architectural forms upon which to base extravagant designs. Egyptomania seized hold of the world a second time when Tutankhamun's mummy embarked on a world tour for much of the 1970s. Design duo Lisa Mayock and Sophie Buhai behind the label Vena Cava took Egyptomania's 1970s incarnation as a cue for their Spring/Summer 2009 collection. They turned out

70s-style sportswear sets printed with hieroglyphs and astrological symbols, and the finale look was an evening gown covered in excerpts from an Egyptian glossary on ancient mythology.

In recent centuries Egypt has been under the control of various world powers, whose governing elites have served as major influences on styles of clothing. Regrettably, as long as Egypt was under foreign domination, the country was seen as a source for raw materials and very little manufacturing was fostered. Thus the emergence of a local fashion design industry was kept at bay until independence from Britain was finally achieved in 1954. Even in the 1960s and 1970s stringent economic conditions continued to make fashion goods scarce, and only a small percentage of Egyptians who comprise the wealthy upper class could afford to travel to Europe – or later to Lebanon or Dubai – to buy their clothing.

Egypt had no widely known designers until after 2000, but that is gradually changing and the advent of the internet and the blogosphere has brought fashion to Cairo's doorstep. The capital is now bustling with funky concept stores and luxury boutiques and has

Egyptian designer Marie Bishara Spring/Summer 2009, Paris

Egyptian designer Marie Bishara Spring/Summer 2009, Paris

its own fashion blog, Fashion Threads, detailing the Cairo scene, launched and maintained by financier and part-time fashionista Nadine Sabry.

Talaat Sharkas, Marie Bishara and Mohamed Nahas were among the first to carve out a name for themselves in the Egyptian high fashion scene. Marie Bishara has shown in Paris, but remains true to her Egyptian origins in her designs, often utilizing Pharaonic colours and Egyptian motifs and symbols, such as the ankh or key of life. Young designer Amina Khalil of the brand Amina K studied in London before returning to Egypt to dress Cairo's socialites. 'Egyptian influence with a western twist,' Khalil told *Daily News Egypt* while describing her style. 'I don't want it to be typical Egyptian, as if you're buying it from Khan El-Khalili [a local souk in Cairo] ... I want it to be that but combined with the trends and what is in ... westernized a bit.' In the jewellery arena, Azza Fahmy is an internationally acclaimed designer whose career spans nearly 40 years. She recently collaborated with British brand Preen for their Autumn/Winter 2010 runway collection in New York.

In recent years, the Egyptian government has recognized the value in cultivating a thriving local fashion industry. The Industrial Modernization Centre and the Ministry of Trade and Industry have launched a series of initiatives to nurture and support young Egyptian talent. As Khalil remarked to *Daily News Egypt* 'It is really picking up as an industry. People are finally seeing the importance of looking nice and dressing up and now they are starting to really have access.'

So as far as fashion is concerned, despite its long and rich history, it is quite possible that Egypt's greatest treasures may not in fact still be lying buried beneath its sands, but instead sit in the capable hands of a new generation of creatives.

RECOMMENDED DESIGNERS AND RESOURCES
Egypt

Marie Bishara
Heba Elawadi
Fashion Threads
Blog http://fashionthreads.wordpress.com

the middle east

Introduction

The Middle East's contribution to world fashion is of wide-reaching historical and current importance. It can be seen in the way light dances through the intricate fretwork of Arab architecture, manifesting in carefully pinched, tucked and twisted fabric appliqué peeking through crop tops worn underneath immaculately tailored blazers or adorning the front side of a pencil skirt on the Preen Spring/Summer 2011 runway at New York Fashion Week; or in the politics of the *keffiyeh* causing a stir on the runways of Paris at Balenciaga Autumn/Winter 2007; or in the spiritual opulence of the Byzantine Empire at Chanel pre-Autumn/Winter 2009 and Alexander McQueen Autumn/Winter 2010; or in the burgeoning new local fashion industry that has sprung up in countries throughout the region.

Though in the West the region has become synonymous above all with political and religious turmoil, it is also the cradle of human civilization, from which have come many of humankind's most profound artistic and architectural achievements. These have provided inspiration for countless modern fashion designers – Givenchy's Riccardo Tisci, Dolce and Gabbana, Betsy Johnson, Christian Dior's John Galliano, and William Tempest are just a few of the names who have shown Middle Eastern-inspired collections in recent years – while the emirate of Dubai has come to epitomize luxury shopping to such an extent that it served as the destination of the holiday-going cast of cult fashionista-obsessed film *Sex and the City 2*. The region is also home to some of the best-loved names in the industry: from Israel comes Lanvin Creative Director Alber Elbaz; from Beirut, titans of the red carpet Zuhair Murad, Reem Acra, Elie Saab and Georges Chakra; and from Turkey, home of the harem trouser, come Rıfat Özbek and Dice Kayekm, and from Turkish Cyprus Hussein Chalayan.

Opposite Model displays piece from Karl Lagerfeld's Byzantium inspired collection for Chanel at the Metiers d'Art Pre-Fall collection show 2010, Paris

Turkish Cypriot designer Hussein Chalayan Autumn/Winter 2002, Paris

Model wearing Hussein Chalayan Autumn/Winter 2007, Paris

'There's a very sophisticated Middle Eastern client who wants the very best in footwear for every occasion and they want it presented [in] a space that resonates with the new world that is fast emerging in the Middle East.'

Few articles of clothing speak as clearly around the world as the *burqa*. A loose, body-enveloping outer garment worn by many Islamic women to cover their bodies whilst outside their homes, the *burqa* has become an intriguing sartorial symbol which, due to Arab women's keen love of luxury, has made as strong a fashion statement as it does a political one. For many in the non-Muslim world, the *burqa*, the act of veiling and the *hijab*, or Islamic dress in general, conjure up negative images of the oppression of women by Islamic extremists, in particular by the Taliban who ruled Afghanistan from 1996 to 2001. But for others the *hijab* and the *burqa* merely denote cultural and spiritual beauty, not to mention all the glitz and glamour of a rapidly blossoming Muslim

fashion industry (estimated to be worth more than US$96 billion) which thrives on creating exquisite couture and couture-like garments whilst preserving a woman's modesty. And for internationally renowned fashion designers, showing on the runways of Paris and London, such as the avant-garde Hussein Chalayan, whose Spring/Summer 1998 collection presented six models in various states of immodesty, from fully veiled and berobed to veiled but otherwise completely naked, Islamic dress offers a well of inspiration from which to create powerful and artistic high fashion.

Though a Western perspective may view the Islamic mentality of modesty and veiling as potentially inhibiting a woman's wardrobe, the specific niche created by fashion aficionados of the Islamic faith spawned a self-sufficient fashion industry all of its own. The discovery of oil in the region (especially the Arabian Peninsula) prior to the Second World War created vast wealth in a relatively short period of time. With cash to burn, urban men and women alike from the likes of Saudi Arabia or the Gulf States could indulge a taste for European luxury and sophistication as exemplified in the clothes of Christian Dior, Ralph Lauren and Yves Saint Laurent. By the 1990s, a new fashion industry aimed at religious women had begun to emerge, offering clothes specifically designed to maintain religious modesty without sacrificing fashionable flair. Even full-body Islamic swimwear was created, dubbed the 'burqini', which has since hit the runway at Dubai Fashion Week and now sells in over 30 countries.

In recent years, the European and American fashion houses have sunk roots in the Middle East, opening a string of luxury boutiques in places such as Dubai, Abu Dhabi and Beirut. In the summer of 2010 alone, Parisian luxury footwear designer Christian Louboutin and Louis Vuitton both opened stores on exclusive shopping streets in newly reconstructed Beirut.

'The Beirut launch is very significant because there's a very sophisticated Middle Eastern client who wants the very best in footwear for every occasion and they want it presented [in] a space that resonates with the

Models in Anatolian inspired creations by Hussein Chalayan Autumn/Winter 2002, Paris

Portrait of a woman wearing a *Niqaab*

new world that is fast emerging in the Middle East while staying true to their customs,' commented Christian Louboutin in a press release at the time of the launch.

> ***'Some women in Saudi Arabia don't want to feel obliged to wear the*** *abaya*. ***They want to wear it to look fashionable, as well.'***

Not only did these luxury brands expand to embrace the Muslim market, they also began to re-evaluate their merchandise to cater specifically to it, including releasing a slew of exclusive and expensive limited-edition scarves, handbags and jewellery. *Abayas*, the floor-length body-covering black robes Muslim women don over their clothing in public, have blossomed into a fashion force unto themselves. Transformed by the hands of young designers and couturiers, *abayas* can retail for up to US$10,000; the garment has truly evolved from its original conservative function into a piece of high fashion. *Abayas* today come in a variety of colours in addition to the traditional black, in luxurious fabrics and with

embellishments. Many are made to order as stylish Muslim women often want to match their French or Italian designer accessories to their *abayas*. Now these garments are also for sale in London's Harrods where the DAS Collection designed by sister duo Hind and Reem Beljafla hit the shop floor one month after Qatar's sovereign-wealth fund bought the historic Knightsbridge store.

In 2009, Saks Fifth Avenue hosted a couture show in Paris in which top European designers created one-off made-to-measure *abayas*. Amongst them were John Galliano, Nina Ricci, Carolina Herrera, and Italian houses Blumarine and Alberta Ferretti. Members of the Saudi royal family were in attendance as the venue, the lavish Hotel George V, is owned by Saudi Prince Al-Waleed bin Talal.

"'I realised that most of the Saudi clients are wearing designer brands, but they're covered by a black *abaya*,"' Dania Tarhini, the show's organiser and a general manager of Saks Fifth Avenue in Saudi

Turkish carpets

Arabia, told the *Telegraph* at the time of the event. "'It is an obligation to wear the *abaya* there, but some women in Saudi Arabia don't want to feel obliged to wear the *abaya*. They want to wear it to look fashionable, as well.'"

All this interest in Western fashions was not without a matched, burgeoning interest amongst young local designers adapting Western forms to local needs, thus spawning a regionally specific and unique fashion industry. Some fashion designers have opted to follow purely Western styles of garment, to create new designs based on such trends and eventually to show abroad – for instance, red-carpet king and designer friend to Hollywood's A-list, Beirut-born Elie Saab, who is based in Paris. Other designers with cultural connections to the region have decided to create contemporary looks based on traditional and regional textiles and fashion styles. Some, such as Turkish-born Rifat Özbek and Dice Kayek and the Turkish Cypriot Chalayan, use a mixture of Turkish and Western cuts and textiles.

A new wave of fashion media, both a budding blogosphere and the advent of major glossy publications such as *Vogue Turkey* and *Grazia Middle East*, has given a platform to a new generation of talented young designers. But it is not out of nowhere that this new era of modesty-conscious designers has sprung up in the region; they come in response to a growing clamour from a generation of young Muslims, citizens of the 21st century, trying to re-establish their identity in a post-9/11 political climate. "'Our generation became more aware of their identity when [we] were thrust into the limelight after 9/11 and 7/7 and other events of the past decade or so,'" remarked Jana Kossaibati, British blogger and founder of Muslim fashion website Hijab Style, to the BBC in 2010. "'We were forced to deal with people questioning our faith, our identity and the way we look. Young Muslims are increasingly looking for fashion that doesn't set them apart from the rest of society.'"

Models promoting the first Israeli Fashion Week 2004

Israel

A holy land to three of the world's major religions, Israel is also a breeding ground for another kind of icon. From this small but significant country hail the likes of supermodel Bar Refaeli and Lanvin Creative Director Alber Elbaz as well as super-luxe swimwear brand Gottex. But the fruitful fashion industry of today's Israel has been a long time coming; it took all the years from the formation of the state of Israel in 1948 until the 1990s to find a solid footing, with the successful creation of a distinctively Israeli style mostly characterized by a love of technology and innovative fabrics. So at last it seems, after decades of ups and downs, Tel Aviv, with one of the most eclectic and influential street-style scenes on the planet and a repertoire of exciting young talented designers, is poised for a long tenure as one of the leading fashion capitals in the region.

The development of a fashion industry in what is now the state of Israel dates back to the initial period of Jewish settlement in what was then known as Palestine, at the end of the 19th and the beginning of the 20th centuries. Immigrants from Europe brought with them a Western awareness of fashion trends, particularly orientalism with its emphasis on the exoticism of the East, which was all the rage in Paris at the time.

The mid-1920s saw another wave of Jewish immigration, predominantly from Poland and in particular from Łódź, a textile city. Numbering high amongst these immigrants were the textile professionals who would start the textile and clothing industry in Tel Aviv. Within a few years the city enjoyed a bustling, urban lifestyle, and its wealthy residents, clad in the latest Parisian fashion, had totally abandoned the oriental style. Inhabitants of other cities in Palestine soon followed suit, slipping into Western garb and way of life.

From 1929–39, approximately 250,000 Jews immigrated into British-controlled Palestine, swelling the population by a third. The first immigrants were wealthy Jews of German and Austrian descent, bringing with them new fashion influences from the heart of Europe. Despite the sweltering summer heat, the new Tel Avivans insisted on decking themselves out exactly as they had in Vienna or Berlin. The women swathed themselves in elegant Western-style tailored suits, high-heeled shoes with matching handbags, and even gloves. The men wore suits and ties. These immigrants and their passion for dressing well were the driving force behind the establishment of trendy clothing shops and salons in the city. Mirroring the style of Hollywood and European high society, Tel Aviv nightlife of the 1930s included many crowded parties and glamorous events where men elegantly attired in tuxedos would accompany women decked out in long, backless evening gowns.

The peak of this new industry's success came at the beginning of the Second World War, when many buyers accustomed to purchasing in Germany or Austria before the outbreak of war came to Tel Aviv to buy from the same manufacturers with whom they had been acquainted before the war. From the beginning of 1941 until the end of 1945, fashion weeks were held in Tel Aviv twice a year, making it one of Western Asia's premier fashion

capitals. The Arab states that had stopped buying in Palestine at the beginning of the 1930s for political reasons once again returned to Tel Aviv during the war. They were soon joined by keen retailers from Cyprus, Iran and Turkey.

During the years 1948–60, hundreds of thousands of immigrants were absorbed into Israel, and the population doubled. The young Israeli government, having seized power by force after the Second World War, and suddenly faced with having to create jobs, launched Maskit, a project geared toward the preservation of the ethnic handicrafts brought by the immigrants and their incorporation into commercial fashion products for sale on the local market. Maskit thus became the melting pot for Israeli fashion. It succeeded in combining the traditional handicrafts of Jews from Morocco, Iraq, Kurdistan, Yemen and Bukhara in Uzbekistan with the modern, up-to-date vision of its head designer, Fini Leitersdorf.

Ossie Clark Spring/Summer 2009, London

Ossie Clark Spring/Summer 2009, London

Model in a swimsuit by Gottex Spring/Summer 2010, New York

'It's a fusion of technology and luxury, created to accentuate the female form.'

Leitersdorf's iconic Desert Coat was the ultimate Israeli sartorial creation, in which fashion and folklore were perfectly combined. A hand-woven garment of roughly textured sheep's wool cut from one piece of fabric, the coat draped diagonally over the body and was considered the faithful ambassador of Israeli fashion for almost three decades.

Despite the success of a few emerging Israeli brands, 1950s Israel was nonetheless a time characterized by severity, restricted by the austerity regime of the time. The regime provided each citizen with a book of coupons, commonly known as points. These were the only way of buying clothes, food or household items. The brand Lakol (meaning 'suitable for all without discrimination') was introduced to produce a range of basic textile products. There was a sudden craze for all things khaki, and 'biblical' sandals (strappy flats made of two parallel strips of leather across the instep, with a strap around the ankle) became the go-to footwear for people across all walks of Israeli life, as they were cheap, practical and comfortable, and could be purchased for a minimal number of points. The combination of khaki and biblical sandals, worn by the 'Sabras', a term describing those Israelis born in Israeli territory, was the unofficial uniform for the young generation who had fought for the birth of modern Israel, and served as an ideological tool for the young regime struggling to build the new state.

As with the rest of the Western world austerity in Israel ended with the 1960s. With improved economic circumstances came a new awareness of fashion trends that were a far cry from the purposely drab, monotonous and khaki-crazed 1950s. Israelis could now afford to travel abroad, and they returned with the latest fashions, which at the time meant miniskirts and jeans. Israeli society, which was young and dynamic, took note of the fashion innovations of the times and immediately embraced them. Ultra-miniskirts and the geometric hair designs of Vidal Sassoon were all the rage in the streets of Tel Aviv. Tiny, dark boutiques sprang up on Dizengoff Street in Tel Aviv, stocking clothes mostly imported from Paris and London or

Model in a swimsuit by Gottex Spring/Summer 2010, New York

designed by young local Israeli fashion designers taking their first tentative steps into the world of fashion.

The original Israeli look first developed in the 1960s drew inspiration from the clothing of the ancient Hebrews. Attempts to explore ancient Hebrew dress resulted in the so-called Ein Gedi model, which was made of fabric woven according to an ancient motif copied from a piece of fabric from the second century ad that was discovered in the caves at Ein Gedi in the Judaean Desert. The garment was presented in two designs. The first was a sleeveless wool dress with fringed edges and a large fringed shawl. The second was similar to the first, but with a coarser look and without the fringing. Israeli fashion houses spared no effort in creating original designs that would keep up with international high-fashion innovations, and for a long time they succeeded.

Swimwear designs by Gottex achieved the level of haute couture. The addition of accessories such as beachwear, shoulder capes, pants and blouses by founder and designer Leah Gottleib marked out Gottex swimwear as a lifestyle statement and catapulted the brand to international recognition. With their accent on stylish ethnic motifs and rich embroidery, they were also made of high-quality materials using innovative technology, an aspect of their brand DNA which still typifies their collections today, now designed by London-based Molly Grad. 'The collection celebrates women,' Grad wrote in the show notes of her Spring/Summer 2011 collection. 'It's a fusion of technology and luxury, created to accentuate the female form. Fabrics have been especially developed ranging from ruched Lycra to foiled metal Lycra. Materials used range from lucite, [to] rock crystals to hammered titanium metals and resin rock-like formations.' Gottex continues to show at Mercedes Benz New York Fashion Week each season.

Tel Aviv also secured a niche in the leather goods industry thanks especially to one particular factory, Beged-Or. Located on the periphery of Tel Aviv as part of the Ministry of Trade and Industry's ambitious plan to establish the fashion and textiles industries on the outskirts of the nation's cities, the factory was originally meant to manufacture basic leather coats. But in 1968 the factory was bought by

Alber Elbaz for Lanvin Spring/Summer 2011, Paris

Alber Elbaz for Lanvin Spring/Summer 2011, Paris

Leslie Fulop, who decided to turn it into a modern factory for high fashion. For this purpose he established a research and development department that experimented with sophisticated processes for combining natural and synthetic leather, furs, wool and acrylic, thereby achieving interesting and unique textures never seen before. Indeed, long before the distressed look commandeered the catwalks of the 1990s and 2000s, the company produced jackets and leathers rendered in mottled tortoiseshell and other weathered treatments. In its heyday of the 1960s and 1970s, Beged-Or was regarded as one of the finest leather houses in the world.

One of the noted designers working in Israel at the time was Gideon Oberson, who studied in Paris, and has worked with French couturiers such as Nina Ricci and Pierre Cardin. Apart from the line he has produced for his own swimwear label, Gideon Oberson has also designed collections for other Israeli fashion houses, including a stint at Gottex, earning himself a name as a very stylish and minimalistic designer in tune with international fashion trends.

Penina Shalon emerged as another star around this time, having started out in Maskit as a manual knitting machine instructor before going on to develop knits with unusual textures. Wool, silk, velvet, straw and ribbons were made into thin threads, interwoven with the glittering effects of silver and gold lurex. Her knits appear delicate and personal in the approach, managing to convey a hand-worked look and ageless style.

However, the designers truly responsible for putting Israel on the fashion map were Fini Leitersdorf, with her creations for Maskit, and Roji Ben-Joseph, with her designs for Rikma. Fini Leitersdorf based her designs on motifs of Israeli origin inspired by the landscape, heritage and local materials, imbuing them with a timeless power using haute-couture techniques. Roji Ben-Joseph employed the same sources of inspiration but created designs for mass production. Fini Leitersdorf's garments were made of silk and pure wool, with silver accessories, while Roji Ben-Joseph's were made of inexpensive cotton adorned with brilliant-coloured stripes or with the addition of printed oriental motifs and macramé knots. While Maskit items were very expensive and far beyond the reach of most people, the Rikma items were reasonably priced and affordable.

The energy crisis that followed the Yom Kippur War in 1973 resulted in a waning demand for Israeli fashion garments abroad. In an attempt to survive in the changing international fashion market, various experiments were made to create a new definitive Israeli style that would revive the golden touch of the

Young Israelis at the annual Gay Pride parade in Tel Aviv, 2009

Model Bar Refaeli for Louis Vuitton Autumn/Winter 2010, Paris

1960s. But these experiments failed to bring back to Israeli fashion the prestige and high demand that had characterized it in the preceding decade. The textile factories that had once exported high-priced, top-quality fashion abroad now manufactured as subcontractors for cheap fashion chains or for catalogues. Israeli fashion became indistinguishable from global fashion, and all attempts to bring to it a unique look failed.

In this period, Israeli fashion magazines reflect the flat state of the industry. Gone was the former originality, which had been due in part to the use of local ethnic motifs, innovative fabrics and historical inspirations. All attempts to create an original Israeli fashion line ceased, with the aim becoming solely to manufacture standard, reasonably priced fashion goods in accordance with international trends. Foreign buyers who came to the fashion week in Israel found themselves disappointed because, instead of alighting upon unique Israeli style, instead they were greeted by ubiquitous globalized fashions that could be found elsewhere at cheaper prices.

Starting in the mid-1980s, Israeli fashion weeks were cancelled due to low interest from buyers. In this atmosphere of indisputable mediocrity, young designers sank into mundane, mass-produced lines, losing their originality.

But from the ashes rises the fashion phoenix, and Israel was not immune to the contagion of fashion that exploded in the 1990s, with the dawn of the era of the supermodel and the birth of fast fashions. Once again, the streets of Tel Aviv were bubbling with vitality, enlivened with the latest fashion novelties, with a decidedly strong leaning toward the fashions of London and Japan. Young Israelis with fashion awareness styled themselves in eccentric outfits created from second-hand garments. Rumours of this novel street fashion scene rapidly attracted the attention of the hosts of popular television shows such as those produced by the Canadian TV channel Fashion Television or the popular music channel MTV, which in the late 1990s sent fashion reporters to Israel to cover its fashion scene.

Today, Tel Aviv has become a force in the realm of global street fashion, with a slew of hit blogs like The Streetwalker and ILook. While ILook captures more of the punky, statement-making edge of the street folk or the girl-next-door who throws on a pair of green leggings but still manages to look ever so stylish as she walks out of the door, The Streetwalker goes for the more classic and trendy, but slightly offbeat style of Israeli locals. Nimi Aviga, the photographer behind ILook, has since relocated to London, and runs a site called Style Tube.

> *'Israeli fashion is as good as any in Paris or Milan.'*

Alongside the global trends dominating Israeli fashion from the 1990s through to the present day, a wave of new and refreshing designs by young designers – mainly graduates of the Shenkar College of Textile Technology and Fashion– filtered into the market. Although influenced by international trends, these young designers sought a unique path of their own within the global context. Some of them opened small studios, mostly at the northern end of Dizengoff and nearby streets in Tel Aviv. These designers stood out in international fashion competitions, where they were frequently awarded first prizes and received high acclaim. Some of the talented young designers went abroad, where they acquired international reputations: Among them were Alber Elbaz, who became Artistic Director for Lanvin in Paris in 2001, and Avsh Alom Gur, appointed Creative Director for the revived Ossie Clark label in London, while maintaining his own eponymous label. Alber Elbaz was born in Casablanca, Morocco, but moved to Tel Aviv at the age of ten and considers himself Israeli. He is credited with reversing the fortunes of Lanvin, one of the oldest of the classic French fashion houses, breathing new life into a moribund but still revered name and transforming it into one of the most coveted luxury brands worldwide, whose influence can often be felt trickling down to the high street and mass market.

The phenomenon of these up-and-coming young designers gathered momentum in 2000, when they suggested an interesting alternative to popular global fashion. Tel Aviv held its first official new fashion week in 2009, and the same year a group of Israel's top designers presented their collections in a showcase at Los Angeles Fashion Week.

In 2003, former Macy's buyer Fern Penn opened the first collective shop in New York to feature solely Israeli designers. The Soho-based store, named Rosebud, showcases the fashion and homewares of more than 20 Israeli designers, amongst which are the popular silk dresses of Katomenta, tote bags by Kisim (as spotted on the arm of Sarah Jessica Parker in *Sex and the City: The Movie*), and separates by Ronen Chen and Hagit Witman.

'"It's a concept store,"' explained Fern Penn to Israeli news website ISRAEL21c around the time of the launch in 2003. '"Israeli fashion is as good as any in Paris or Milan. Our point is to show people that Israeli fashion is not what you think – it doesn't have to be ethnic – it can be elegant."'

It's clear from Penn's confident statement that the Israeli fashion scene is currently thriving, having found an authentic, durable style in the daily choices of young urban Tel Avivans as well as the energetic ideas of numerous Israeli designers. It's a far cry from khaki and sandals!

RECOMMENDED DESIGNERS AND RESOURCES
Israel

Ronen Chen
Mirit Weinstock
Yigal Azrouel
http://www.yigal-azrouel.com

Three men wearing red and white colored turbans

Palestine

Why, you may be asking, is the author writing a chapter on a country that no longer exists? Well, though it is yet to be recognised by the powerful Western member nations of the UN, to the majority of Arab states and to many other countries across the world, the right of the Palestinian people to a homeland is self-evident. It is also true to say that the denial of that right has led to 60 years of conflict in the region, whose repercussions continue to be felt across the globe.

The Palestinian people – those who are not crammed uncomfortably into the Palestinian territories within Israel itself – are scattered in a global diaspora, but particularly in neighbouring countries such as Jordan and Syria, which absorbed millions of Palestinian refugees in the years after the Israelis seized control of their former lands in

the late 1940s. Such hardship can crush a people's spirit, but it can also strengthen the determination to preserve their cultural identity, no matter what.

For thousands of years, the former Palestinian lands have been ruled by a variety of different empires and groups, from the ancient Egyptians and the Romans to the Ottomans and finally the British. From the medieval period on, Muslims formed the majority of the population, with Jews and Christians being minority groups. During the 20th century, the term 'Palestine' was used for the area included within the boundaries of British Mandate for Palestine (1922–48), often referred to as the Mandate period. Its western boundary was the Mediterranean Sea, while the eastern boundary was approximately where the Syrian Desert begins.

Model in a traditional Palestinian dress

Following the establishment of the State of Israel in 1948 in the northern, western, and southern parts of Palestine, there was a mass exodus of people, with over half the rural Palestinian population becoming refugees in the Gaza and West Bank areas as well as in neighbouring countries. A second wave of refugees ensued after the Six Day War of 1967 and as a result very little remains of the dress and textile traditions of the 19th and the first half of the 20th century, for which Palestinians were once renowned. Traditional garments, especially dresses, experienced a resurgence after 1967 but in much plainer styles than before, whereas a defining feature of Palestinian dress had been the wide variety of fabrics and materials used to create garments and accessories.

There was a strong local weaving tradition throughout the former Palestine. Indeed the city of Gaza gave its name to gauze, after the fine type of silk, known as *gazzatum*, produced there as early as the 13th century and imported into medieval Europe. Cotton, on the other hand, was cultivated in the Galilee area of former Palestine (or modern-day Israel), dyed blue or black, and then used for everyday dresses. Although Bethlehem, again at one time considered a part of Palestine, produced its own *malak* fabrics (flax and silk threads woven together), linen came from Egypt and Eastern Europe, while a vast array of silk materials came from Syria and Lebanon, in addition to those already mentioned that were produced locally. Embroidery in ancient Palestine is perhaps best known for its cross-stitch patterns in various geometric or floral motifs.

By the mid-19th century, however, the rich world of hand-woven Palestinian textiles and handmade dress had been more or less replaced either by Western styles or Islamic dress. Local weaving practices ceased, and, without access to imported textiles and embroidery threads, traditional dress from the villages and that of the Palestinian Bedouin, lost its stylish nuance and became streamlined for practicality.

During the early 1980s another new form of dress called *shawal* was developed; it was made from pre-embroidered linen which was then sewn onto the main fabric of the dress. These were often sold with a fringed shawl with similarly worked embroidery, creating a set. The main designs were geometric motifs. Although originally designed for the Western market, the *shawal* soon became popular among Arab women throughout the region and has developed into a kind of Palestinian fashion statement and even, as some claim, a manifestation of Palestinian haute couture.

Model in a traditional Palestinian dress

Palestinian leader Yasser Arafat

Palestinian sartorial identity over the last 60 years has of course been profoundly affected by the political struggle of its people. The First Intifada period of the 1987–93 used traditional dress as a means of silent, but effective protest, so that the issue of how you dressed became a matter of national pride. The *shawal* was thus soon recruited to the cause, evolving into a powerful nationalistic icon, the flag dress. These were different from the earlier *shawals* because they used certain nationalistic embroidery motifs like the Palestinian flag or its colours, or maps of Palestine, or slogans such as '*Filasteen*' (the Arabic word for Palestine) or 'PLO'. The flag dresses allowed women to express their own involvement in the Palestinian uprising; they were made and worn purely in symbolic defiance of those they considered their oppressors and did not compromise the everyday garb of women in the refugee camps or the Palestinian territories. In the Palestinian territories of today, most women do not own an embroidered dress, as would have been the case with previous generations, but although embroidery has largely lost its function as an artistic expression of a woman's

identity and skill, it nevertheless remains a powerful expression of Palestinian culture.

But while the notoriety of the flag dress has remained somewhat local, that of its male equivalent, the infamous and celebrated *keffiyeh*, the traditional rectangular checked head cloth worn by men throughout the Arab world, has enjoyed a long and active history of representing, or misrepresenting, the Palestinian cause abroad. In 1936, the Palestinians rebelled against Jewish immigration into Palestine under the British Mandate, and although this revolt was officially led by the urban elite, the armed rebel groups mainly consisted of peasant guerillas who used the *keffiyeh* to hide their faces, preventing identification.

No single fashion accessory in early 21st-century Western society is as political and controversial as the *keffiyeh*. Be it wrapped around the head of the infamous former leader of the Palestine Liberation Organization (PLO) Yasir Arafat, twisted into fringed frocks on the catwalks by Balenciaga's

Nicholas Ghesquière, topping the crowns of a group of gun-toting insurgents or lining sale bins at Topshop or Urban Outfitters, the *keffiyeh* treads the unorthodox line between authentic symbol of opposition to the oppression of the Palestinians and 'it' fashion accessory of the last five to ten years; essentially pointing to the inescapable fact that in this region, even more so than everywhere else in the world, the language of fashion is inextricably bound up with that of politics.

Two individuals were largely responsible for elevating the scarf's status from regional headgear to international political symbol: Yasir Arafat and Leila Khaled. Arafat, as chairman of the PLO and leader of political party Fatah, was from the 1960s onwards an international representative of the Palestinian cause. He wore a black-and-white *keffiyeh* in a very distinctive way, with one point draped into a triangle over the right shoulder, imitating the shape of Palestine itself. Khaled was a member of the Popular Front for the Liberation of Palestine and took part in the airplane hijackings of 1969 and 1970, both meant to gain international attention for the Palestinian cause. In 1970, pictures of her were published wearing a *keffiyeh* as a head covering. Up to this point, the *keffiyeh* had been the prerogative of men, but Khaled's proud adoption of the scarf rendered the scarf an irrefutable symbol of Palestinian resistance regardless of gender, and from the 1960s and 1970s on, the *keffiyeh* became internationally entwined with the Palestinian people.

As a result of media images of *keffiyeh*-clad Palestinian stone throwers, suicide bombers and hijackers, in the West it has since come to be associated with Islamic terrorism. Both in spite of and because of this, the *keffiyeh* still retains tremendous political significance throughout Europe and the United States. In the mid-1960s, the *keffiyeh* could be spotted at antiwar protests across America, at which it was worn as a sign of sympathy for the Palestinian cause – an example of 'activist chic'. In the 1980s, the head covering became associated with the post-punk subculture, especially in big cities like New York and London, a resurgence that coincided with another international terrorism scare. It was precisely because of its established position in Western subculture, the *keffiyeh* gradually lost its original meaning and was no longer considered a political statement. Only during the Gulf War of 1991 did its political meaning briefly flare up again as a sign of political allegiance, when worn by some opposing the war.

With the collapse of the World Trade Center on September 11, 2001, however, the West once again reeled under the fear of the Islamic world and the *keffiyeh* once more became a subject of discussion, this time as an item appearing on some of the world's most prestigious high-fashion catwalks, specifically that of the House of Balenciaga for the Autumn/Winter 2007 season. Designer Nicholas Ghesquière's sartorial stunt sparked outrage, especially given the price tag of his *keffiyeh* – around £3,000. Soon the trend went mainstream – celebrities such as Colin Farrell, Mary Kate Olsen and Kanye West were spotted in the scarves – and modified versions of the check sprang up in every colour variety, from highlighter yellow to electric blue. Also dubbed the 'tablecloth scarf', the trend has met with protest from both Zionists and those who support the restoration of Palestine. Both felt the wearing of this item was an affront to the history and meaning behind the *keffiyeh*, either as a symbol of opposition to the oppression of the Palestinians or as a symbol of anti-Israeli terrorism and the Intifada. It also outraged the American right, mobilized by American anti-terror campaigns, and in 2008 conservative blogger and author Michelle Malkin went so far as to equate the popularization of the *keffiyeh* in fashion with 'modifying Klan-style hoods in Burberry plaid as the next big thing'.

In the early 21st century, Palestinian dress no longer follows a traditional, regional pattern. Since the early 2000s, various groups, as in other parts of the Arab world, have sought to increase the use of *hijab*, or Islamically correct clothing, among Palestinian women. As a result, more and more women can be seen wearing a long, tailored overcoat (sharia dress) with a headscarf. However, pockets of fashion promise are springing up amongst Palestinians in both Syria and Jordan. Drawing on the people's strong history of embroidery and indomitable national pride, there exists the potential that one day Palestinian sartorial culture will blossom in a way that current conditions make almost impossible, with the *keffiyeh* reduced to a fondly remembered icon of a fractured past.

RECOMMENDED DESIGNERS AND RESOURCES
Palestine

Hindi Mahdi
Rami Kashou

Syria

Syrian women are generally known to be quite fashion-conscious compared with some of their Arab neighbours, especially those in the conservative Gulf States. Syria's British-born First Lady, Asma al-Assad, is herself something of a fashion magnet. In 2008, French *Elle* named her international politics' most stylish lady, beating both France's Carla Bruni-Sarkozy and the US's Michelle Obama. Syria's capital, Damascus, boasts a few private modelling agencies, while a handful of annual fashion shows and expensive designer boutiques have recently popped up in affluent parts of the city, catering to an elite that until a few years ago looked to Dubai or Beirut to satisfy their fashion needs. Syrian dress has long been associated with the kaftan as well as a love of heavy, embroidered fabrics such as brocade. This love of richness and detail (Christian Louboutin has sourced brocade for his luxury high heels from Syria) bodes well for a budding fashion scene, both on and off the runway.

> *'People don't dress as free as the Western world but are still experimental with current fashion trends.'*

"Personally, I feel like the Syrian fashion is just only starting," explains Syrian-born, Dubai/London-based blogger Tala Samman of myfashdiary.com. "We don't have fashion schools or courses, so the few that decide to go into fashion end up travelling abroad and starting their line elsewhere. But very talented designers have moved to Dubai and have their ateliers based in Syria. Rami Al Ali, who creates lots of heavy fabric dresses and kaftans, shows at couture week and dresses lots of Arabic celebrities."

Rami Al Ali is amongst a handful of fashion names known outside of the country. His elaborate couture designs are a harmonic blend of Western influences and intricate Eastern exoticism. After working with some of the region's leading fashion houses in Dubai and Beirut, he established his own line in 2001. In 2009, he showed his Damascus Rose collection at the Alta Moda fashion show in Rome, becoming the first Syrian designer to do so. "'I have accumulated a vast visual memory throughout the years I lived in Syria,'"

Ali told online magazine, Dia Boutique, in 2010. "'This comes to the surface creatively in every piece or collection I create. It can be seen in the graphics and colour combinations of my collections. This comes from artwork inspired from the Syrian craftsmanship like the mosaic, the famous multi-ethnic architecture and the traditional or ethnic garments I see.'"

In 2009, Syria held its first-ever fashion design competition, where models clad in backless dresses strutted before an audience of *hijab*-clad Syrian women. Designer Rania Nashawaty's collection included modern, Western-inspired pieces, but also a retake on the flag dress: she created a folkloric dress with the Syrian flag trailing behind as a train. "The show aims for encouraging young Syrian talents and locally made works," young designer Musaab Hureib commented to English People's Daily (an English-language arm of the official Chinese Xinhua news agency) after showing in the 2010 instalment of the competition. "'The svelte models hit the catwalk in attractive bare-back dresses with long hemlines. It is rare to see that in Syria.'"

Indeed, as Samman points out, while Islamic restraint is omnipresent on the streets there, young Syrians find alternative ways to experiment with trends and express themselves. "The street style scene in Syria is quite on trend, and conservative,'" says Samman. "People don't dress as free as the Western world but are still experimental with current fashion trends. But I am hoping that within the next five years, the Syrian fashion industry will open up some doors to the talented local fashion designers, as well as the established multi-brand stores (Aishti and Villa Moda, in particular) start stocking local talent."

RECOMMENDED DESIGNERS AND RESOURCES *Syria*

Rami Al Ali
Rania Nashawaty
Riham Zahreldeen
Musaab Hureib

Opposite Model walks the runway for Syrian designer Rami Al Ali, Spring/Summer 2010, Rome

> *'Any brand looking to truly 'go global' cannot ignore the Middle East.'*

Jordan

Jordan is also home to a number of budding designers and held its first fashion week in the capital city, Amman, in 2008, in an attempt to cater to an emerging luxury market. Jeweller Lama Hourani is perhaps the most successful Jordanian designer abroad. She has been designing since 2000, and in 2004 opened her first gallery and jewellery shop in Amman. Her baubles, inspired by both the natural and cultural landscape of her native Jordan, captured the attention of major fashion press and celebrities alike. She has even designed for Her Majesty Queen Rania of Jordan.

As for ready-to-wear, Intisar Farekh-Khalifeh made a name for herself in the 1980s by reinventing the traditional embroidered ankle-length Palestinian dress, experimenting with bright colour, lightweight fabrics and more risqué silhouettes. Her designs were embraced by the younger generations and worn by the former queen of Jordan, Queen Noor, at public functions around the world. Soon, other princesses and Arab high society from Saudi Arabia, Kuwait, Egypt and Lebanon flocked to Intisar Farekh-Khalifeh's atelier.

Today, Amman is an emerging retail hub, and high-society women who used to look elsewhere for their designer duds are finding more and more places to shop at home. This is true not just for luxury items. The youth of Amman are style-conscious and hungry for trends, and in 2003 the intriguingly named Mecca Mall opened in Amman, heralding a new era of retail consumption in Jordan.

In 2006, American fast-fashion retail chain Forever 21 opened an outpost in the mall. "'Amman is recognised for its fast-growing fashion scene and trend-savvy and fashion-adoptive consumers," the chain's founder, Don Chang, commented at the time to Middle East business website ameinfo.com. "'With a large population of young ladies with an average age of 22 years, it's got the right potential waiting to be tapped and we have no doubt that Amman will soon emerge as one of the fashion capitals in the Middle East. Any brand looking to truly 'go global' cannot ignore the Middle East and to be a major player in the Middle East one cannot ignore Jordan.'"

Queen Noor of Jordan

RECOMMENDED DESIGNERS AND RESOURCES *Jordan*

Nadia Dajani
Lama Hourani
Intisar Farekh-Khalifeh

Lebanon

Lebanon is the region's cradle of couture, the 'Paris of the Middle East' where couturiers seem to grow on trees even amidst civil wars and periods of prolonged political strife. Thanks to a steady influx of tourists and a relatively stable banking system, in the years since 2006, when missiles last ravaged the streets of Beirut during the month-long war between Israel and Hezbollah, Lebanon's cultural affinity for couture has only intensified. With a host of heavyweights dispatched to the four corners of the style globe, names like Elie Saab and Reem Acra, and a new generation of designers and bloggers chomping at the proverbial bit, Beirut has risen in a genuine bid to become the Middle East's fashion epicentre.

Prior to 1918, Lebanon had been under Ottoman rule and influence for four hundred years – a period in which cloth weaving and embroidery flourished. Following the First World War, Lebanon became part of the French Mandate until its independence in 1943. As in the African territories under French colonial tutelage, tailoring and pattern-cutting techniques from the ateliers of Paris were gradually absorbed into the workshops of the local peoples, but traditional dress was slow to change, with aristocrats following the fashions of post-Ottoman Istanbul. Although the introduction of European fashion into the area was at first hesitant, it subsequently succeeded in penetrating the moneyed classes. As a result, surviving examples of traditional dress from this period are rare.

Thanks to its tightly regulated financial system, Lebanese banks have emerged from the global financial crisis of recent years largely unscathed. In fact, in 2009, despite the global recession, Lebanon enjoyed 9% economic growth and welcomed the largest number of tourists in its history. So while high-end fashion suffered from the global downturn, Lebanese haute couture has experienced a kind of

Abed Mahfouz fashion show at AltaRoma AltaModa Autumn/Winter 2010

A model walks for Elie Saab at Paris Haute Couture Fashion Week Autumn/Winter 2011, Paris

rebirth. Clients from the oil rich Gulf drive massive sales of bespoke gowns starting at £15,000. And so, from the conflict ridden yet cosmopolitan streets of Beirut have risen international fashion stars Zuhair Murad, Georges Chakra and Abed Mahfouz, as well as the afore-mentioned Reem Acra and Elie Saab, each of whom have a solid catwalk presence in the West. Indeed, hardly a red carpet in Europe or the US seems quite right without one of their sparkling gowns traversing up and down it.

Of these five, the Paris-based Elie Saab is perhaps the most recognizable name, having dressed celebrities from Elizabeth Hurley to Beyoncé. The self-trained couturier launched his first fashion label in Beirut in 1982 at the age of 18. A decade and a half later, he became the first non-Italian designer to become a member of the Camera Nazionale della Moda, and in 1997 in Rome showed his first collection outside Lebanon. The following year, he launched a ready-to-wear line in Milan, where in 2002 he achieved the accolade of being the first Lebanese designer to

dress an Oscar winner, Halle Berry, after she wore his aubergine silk and embroidered floral creation to collect her statuette for Best Actress that year. In 2003, the French Chambre Syndicale de la Haute Couture invited him to become a member, and he showed his first haute couture collection in Paris in July of that year. His first ready-to-wear collection in Paris was the Spring/Summer 2006 collection, and the city is now his permanent ready-to-wear runway.

Reem Acra meanwhile is renowned in the US for her regal bridal designs, and for dressing film stars Kate Beckinsale and Eva Longoria Parker as well as Jill Biden, the wife of the US Vice President, Joe Biden. While attending the American University of Beirut in the 1990s, Reem Acra was discovered by a visiting fashion editor who, captivated by the ornately embroidered silk organza gown she had made from her mother's dining-room tablecloth to wear to a party, instantly offered to host a fashion show of Acra's designs, which took place ten days later. Off the success of that show, she took

Zuhair Murad for Paris Haute Couture Fashion Week
Autumn/Winter 2007

Reem Acra Spring/Summer 2009, New York

up a place at the prestigious Fashion Institute of Technology in New York and went on to study at Esmod Paris. Like Elie Saab, Reem Acra's aesthetic is rooted in a harmonious blend of vibrant Eastern influences with a western understanding of cut, silhouette and luxury.

Zuhair Murad opened his first atelier in Beirut in 1995 and shot quickly to sartorial stardom with a style he himself describes as a 'charming and innovative mix of Eastern suggestions and a European sensibility for cuts and sartorial styling'. Within five years of cutting his first toile, Zuhair Murad found himself invited to showcase his collection during Alta Roma Alta Moda, and in 2001 presented his first couture collection in Paris. His designs are characterized by a fluidity of silhouette and fairytale-like ornate detail, embroidery and embellishment. In 2010 he received the ultimate seal of fashion approval when Jennifer Lopez donned one of his princess gowns to

the sartorial event of the season, the Metropolitan Museum's Costume Institute Gala. Today Murad has a couture collection and a high-end ready-to-wear line, as well as a collaborative collection with Spanish high-street retailer Mango, called Mango by Zuhair Murad.

Georges Chakra began his career in 1985 by customizing gowns for regional clients, but it was not until 2001 that he made the leap into the realm of international haute couture when he first debuted collections at Paris Fashion Week. Since then, he has gone on to dress the likes of Rihanna and Tyra Banks, had his work featured in major fashion magazines such as *InStyle*, *Elle* and *Harper's Bazaar*, and even outfitted Meryl Streep for the iconic 2006 fashion flick *The Devil Wears Prada*. He now shows his ready-to-wear line, Edition by Georges Chakra, in New York.

Model backstage for Zuhair Murad's Haute Couture show, Spring/Summer 2011, Paris

Abed Mahfouz fashion show at AltaRoma AltaModa Autumn/Winter 2010

While these designers are busy establishing a precedent for Lebanese fashion abroad, back home the streets of Beirut are being rebuilt with luxury fashion as part of the city's infrastructure. In the summer of 2010, Louis Vuitton opened a beautiful store in the Beirut Souks, one of the fastest growing commercial and lifestyle centres in Lebanon, recently rebuilt as a modern hub of luxury shopping to cater more directly to the ever-growing number of loyal Lebanese customers. According to Beirutnightlife.com, Yves Carcelle, Chairman & CEO of Louis Vuitton, at the time of the opening described Beirut as being '"a fascinating city which attracts visitors from not only nearby regions, but the world over"'. Alongside Vuitton, Christian Louboutin was quick to welcome customers into his new concept store, also located in the Beirut Souks. 'The Beirut launch is very significant because there's a very sophisticated Middle Eastern client who wants the very best in footwear for every occasion and they want it

presented in a space that resonates with the new world that is fast emerging in the Middle East while staying true to their customs,' remarked the shoe designer in the press release for the store's launch.

A younger generation also nips at the heels of the great Lebanese couturiers, guaranteeing that the Lebanese passion for fashion will be more than a fleeting phase or a fluke. Young couture house Basil Soda has shown to great acclaim on the runways of Paris, and in 2009 opened a glossy flagship store back home. Blogs have also emerged in Lebanon, the most successful of these being LebFashion.

RECOMMENDED DESIGNERS AND RESOURCES *Lebanon*

Elie Saab
Abed Mahfouz

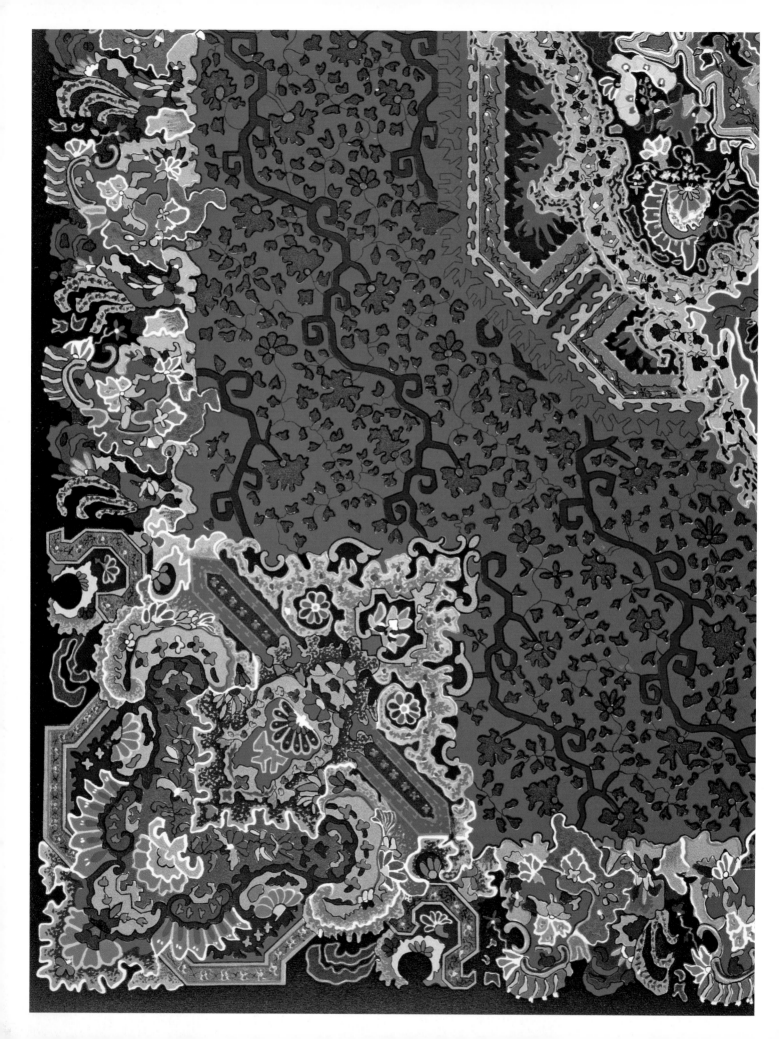

Turkey

Istanbul, Constantinople, Byzantium: one city, many names, its neighbourhoods straddling two continents divided at the banks of the Bosphorus. The heart of the Byzantine Empire and later the Ottoman Empire, Turkey, at the crossroads of Asia and Europe, has for a thousand years been a dynamic player in the great game of world history, with a long, rich history of dress to bear witness to this involvement. From its jewel-bedecked, sable-wrapped sultans luxuriating in the Topkapi Palace to the harem trousers gifted to idle European ladies in the early 1900s, to the politically charged 21st-century avant-garde runway shows of designer Hussein Chalayan, Turkey has one of Western Asia's greatest sartorial traditions.

The Byzantine Empire (or Eastern Roman Empire) was the Roman Empire as it existed during the Middle Ages after the fall of Rome in the West. It was centred on the capital of Constantinople, and ruled by the Byzantine Emperors. The Byzantine economy was among the most advanced in Europe and the Mediterranean for many centuries. Constantinople was a prime hub in a trading network that at various times extended across nearly all of Eurasia and North Africa, in particular being the primary western terminus of the famous Silk Road, the network of trade routes that stretched across the Asian continent all the way to China. Some scholars argue that, up until the arrival of the Arabs in the 7th century, the Empire had the most powerful

Opposite Colour plate showing detail of Turkish rug
Top Women in a Turkish Harem c. 1920

Model displays piece from Karl Lagerfeld's Byzantium inspired collection for Chanel at the Metiers d'Art Pre-Fall collection show 2010, Paris

Model wears Byzantine headdress at Jean Paul Gaultier Spring/Summer 2007 Haute Couture, Paris

economy in the world and accordingly its artistic tradition is amongst the most ornate and splendid in human history. Renowned for its heavy gilding and religious iconography, Byzantine art and the long tradition of Byzantine jewellery have served as a font of inspiration for many fashion designers. Karl Lagerfeld for Chanel pre-Autumn 2009 bedecked his outfits with Byzantine-inspired jewellery, while Jean Paul Gaultier also looked to the splendour of Byzantine jewellery for his Spring/Summer 2007 show in Paris. Veronica Etro, for Etro's Autumn/ Winter 2009 collection shown in Milan, culled inspiration from a Byzantine and Ottoman exhibition she saw at the Royal Academy of Arts in London. Models turned Byzantine icons snaked down the runway in a glittering array of sumptuous golds, burnt bronzes and shimmering coppers adorned with intricate décolletage. Alexander McQueen, in the last collection he designed (Autumn/Winter 2010) before his tragic death last year, recreated the

glory of the empire in exquisite detail through rich embroidery, trumpet sleeves and sumptuous fabric – a Byzantine empress brought to life in fabric.

The Ottoman Empire was at the centre of interactions between the Eastern and Western worlds for six centuries and was, in many respects, an Islamic successor to earlier Mediterranean empires. Turkish culture owes its uniqueness to the absorbed cultures of the people conquered by the Ottomans. But just as Ottoman society was influenced by the decadence of its European neighbours, it was also influenced to a great extent by the more restrained traditions and languages of the Arabic and Persian worlds. These cross-cultural influences from across an Empire which, at its height, stretched from Baku in the east to the horn of Africa in the south, beyond Algiers in the west and almost to Vienna in the north, had an enriching effect on Turkish culture and modes of dress.

The Topkapi Palace in Istanbul, home to a vast collection of opulent Ottoman apparel, is testament to this fact. There are many garments in the collection, ranging from kaftans to stockings; clothes were extremely important to the Ottoman sultans (as they are to most temporal rulers), who wore decadent robes and kaftans sewn of the most expensive and luxurious fabrics. In fact, without their extravagant taste for luxury and exacting demands for superior-quality materials, Ottoman textile weaving (which still serves to inspire many a knitwear collection) would never have developed as magnificently as it did. In the 16th century, for example, gold and silver threads were added to silk textiles. The fame of these silks began to spread, and soon orders for textiles poured into the workshops of Bursa and Istanbul from abroad. Even today, designers such as Matthew Williamson flock to Istanbul to wander its streets, probing its Grand Bazaar for inspiration, which often comes in the form of textiles. Anna Sui (Spring/Summer 2007), Etro (Autumn/Winter 2007), John Galliano (Autumn/Winter 2007), Prada (Spring/Summer 2002) and Ashish Gupta (Autumn/Winter 2010) have all gleaned inspiration from the intricacies of the Turkish rug, its rich colours and complex patterns.

The Ottoman sultans also amassed an impressive collection of furs and wild-animal skins, such as those of the leopard, which have gone on to colour the imaginations of their designer descendants. Contemporary Turkish designer Arzu Karpol, born in Bursa, a Turkish city that was once the capital of the Empire, looks to recreate the subtlety of Ottoman luxury, focusing on details hidden inside the garments, such as fur linings. This attention to detail on Karpol's part recalls to the Ottoman fashion faux pas of wearing fur on the outside of a garment–fur was used as lining only. When the fashion for wearing fur as an outer covering began, the pioneers of the trend became objects of ridicule and were satirized in poems.

Anatolian musicians and dancers in traditional costume at Topkapi Palace, Istanbul

John Galliano Autumn/Winter 2007, Paris

In addition to providing warmth against the harsh Turkish winters, the sultans' fur habit also stemmed from a belief that shamans could transform themselves into animal form or be transported to the heavens by animals. Leopard skins were in widespread use in the Ottoman Palace, particularly spread out on either side of the throne, and represented the protective spirit of the sovereign. Contemporary Turkish designer Rıfat Özbek for his Autumn/Winter 2006 collection looked to the riches of his own Ottoman ancestry for inspiration; in addition to the Ottoman motifs, embroideries and patterns, he embellished his designs with luxurious fur-trimmed collars and cuffs. He also reinterpreted the kaftan with coats in short, modern silhouettes.

While the kaftan may have originated in Mesopotamia and is found in the wardrobes of many cultures, it nevertheless has a revered place in the Turkish tradition, with its own regional nuances to distinguish it from its North African, West African, Indian and Persian counterparts. In fact, notwithstanding the regional diversity of the garment, the word itself actually came into the English language in the late 16th century when it was introduced as the Turkish term to describe the long, formal coats worn in the Ottoman Court. The design of the classic Ottoman kaftan is related to the loom width, with narrow panels of cloth seamed in the centre back, while the garment is open down the centre front. Whilst at the helm of Italian label Pollini, Rifat Özbek directly referenced 16th and 17th century kaftans that had been on display

Oriental evening outfit of full bodied black satin harem pants, gathered at the ankle and topped by square bustier with fake fur by Rifat Özbek for Autumn/Winter 1995

Model in creation by Turkish designer Rifat Özbek for Pollini Spring/Summer 2008, Milan

Karen Elson wearing Anne Sui Spring/Summer 2007, New York

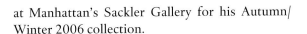
Ashish Autumn/Winter 2010, London

at Manhattan's Sackler Gallery for his Autumn/ Winter 2006 collection.

Kaftan-like garments first began to appear in Western dress during the later Crusades, among clerics who perhaps donned them proudly, as a tourist would a t-shirt, as a token of their pilgrimage to the Holy Land. The association of the kaftan with scholars led to its widespread use as an academic robe that is still worn in university contexts at graduation ceremonies around the world today. Kaftans and kaftan-like garments have continued to appear in Western fashion, notably in the later 20th century. In the 1950s, Christian Dior showed versions of the kaftan without the sash, worn over floor-length evening gowns and perhaps alluding to the 17th century in Europe, where the kaftan (known as the banyan or dressing gown) had its moment in the sartorial spotlight. Both Halston and Yves Saint Laurent followed suit in experimenting with the kaftan in the 1960s, and in the 1970s kaftans

became popular as eveningwear. Simultaneously, throughout the 1960s and 1970s, as the Civil Rights Movement rocked the United States, there was a widespread adoption of African styles of dress–in particular within the African-American community but also, to show support for the cause, in Western fashion at large. The go-to garment of choice among these millions of supporters was the kaftan.

By the 18th century the Ottoman Empire was in decline and, following a prolonged period of increasing chaos and violence in the later 19th century, the Ottoman Empire finally fell at the end of the First World War in a war of independence from which a new Turkish leadership emerged. A treaty signed by both Turkish leaders and European powers partitioned the Ottoman Empire into a new set of countries, most of which had never previously existed as independent states: Iraq, Syria, Lebanon, Palestine, Saudi Arabia, Egypt and Turkey.

The Republic of Turkey was founded on secular principles derived from European and American ideas of social order. The new leaders of this republic, under the founder of the Republic and its first president, Mustafa Kemal Atatürk, believed that the westernizing and secularizing this Muslim society were essential to its becoming a modern nation state, and so Turkey was established with a secular constitution and a secular dress code. Men were immediately encouraged to swap their style of dress and all members of the new government appeared kitted out in Western suits, ties and brimmed fedora hats. In 1925, the fez was banned. Hussein Chalayan's Autumn/Winter 2004 collection, Anthropology of Solitude, touches on just such a moment in Turkish history. Because the dress of women was a more controversial issue, there was no legal ban on the veil or any other aspect of women's dress. For the most part, urban-dwelling women adopted Western styles, but more conservative women in rural areas continued to wear a headscarf on the street.

In the 1980s, a long period of warfare, insurgency and terrorism decimated eastern Turkey, which had remained the most impoverished part of the country. As a result, there was a massive migration of rural villagers to the urban centres of in the west of the country. The more traditionalist populations newly arrived in the cities clashed with the prevailing secularist culture, with the result that the controversy over veiling and conservative Islamic norms of dress has been revived, even though the Turkish constitution still prohibits the wearing of any symbols of religious belief in government offices or institutions, including schools.

An interesting side effect, as it were, of this recrudescence of Islamic culture in Turkey was the

Bora Aksu Spring/Summer 2007, London

Model walks the runway for Turkish designer Rifat Özbek for Pollini Autumn/Winter 2004, Milan

Models display Etro's Autumn/Winter 2009 collection, Milan

Etro Autumn/Winter 2009, Milan

emergence of a new mass-fashion style alongside it, similar to that in other parts of the Islamic world. In the 1980s, for the most part, religious women dressed no differently from secularized women, except for the headscarf. But by the 1990s, a new fashion industry specifically targeting religious women had begun to emerge. Pantsuits, wedding dresses, even swimwear for the covered woman appeared, specially designed to preserve a woman's religious modesty whilst still allowing her to express a bit of personal style. This new apparel also included novel forms of *hijab* headgear designed to match. Today, the streets of Turkey are an eclectic mishmash of styles, cultures, beliefs and ideologies, just as they were at the height of the Ottoman Empire: fashionable professionals walk alongside working-class people in shirts and modern trousers and housewives in tailored skirts and headscarves; while, at the extreme edges, women completely veiled mingle with denim-clad teenage girls and boys.

Over the last two decades, a few expatriate Turkish designers have become international names, in particular Rıfat Özbek, Dice Kayek and, most famously, Turkish Cypriot Hussein Chalayan. These three have gained attention for the universal appeal of their work and have started blending their understanding of modern fashion with their own culture to create a new Turkish design aesthetic. Other important fashion designers working in Turkey include Cemil İpekçi and Yıldırım Mayruk, while a new generation of rising designers includes the already-mentioned Arzu Karpol, among many others.

The most important designer from the region is, of course, Hussein Chalayan, who was born in the Turkish part of Cyprus but graduated from Central Saint Martins in London in 1993. The patriarch of modern conceptual design, even called by some 'the postmodern designer', Chalayan's work bridges

Hussein Chalayan
Autumn/Winter
2010, Paris

Hussein Chalayan Spring/Summer 2009, Paris

Hussein Chalayan Autumn/Winter 2007, Paris

the gap between countries, cultures, regions and religions. The main characteristic of the designer's collections is change; he is constantly seeking his own identity through that of his culture in his garments.

Hussein Chalayan's Between collection (Spring/Summer 1998) brought traditional Islamic dress to the runways of London. One of the designs featured a model clad in a simple red dress but with an egg-shaped wooden capsule entirely covering her head, with only a fine slit for her eyes. While the strange and cumbersome head-covering deprived the model of her individuality, it also provided her with a hard-shelled protection, alluding to the double-edged nature of Islamic dress. Following this disturbing image of womanhood, he sent six models onto the catwalk wearing black chadors of varying lengths and nothing else underneath, exploring the capacity of traditional dress to define and de-individuate the body as it concealed the wearer's identity. The

shortest chador exposed the lower half of the model's body, while another roamed the catwalk in only a *yashmak* (a full-face veil). Similar to the effect the *burqa* must have for the wearer, Hussein Chalayan's veils would have enabled the models to gauge the audience's reactions whilst simultaneously remaining entirely anonymous to the onlookers.

Collections such as the groundbreaking After Words (Autumn/Winter 2000) heightened awareness of the tensions that have resulted in conflicts between Muslims and Christians. After Words referenced the 1974 Turkish military invasion of Cyprus, which displaced both Turkish and Greek Cypriots from their homes. The collection was intended to express displacement and expatriation, the sad reality of people returning in secret to their homes to gather their possessions. Models dressed in simple slips enacted this sad ritual as they removed covers from chairs so as to wear them as dresses. A coffee table became the infamous 'table skirt', while furniture frames folded up into suitcases. By the time the girls had finished, the room was empty.

Ambimorphous (Autumn/Winter 2002) showcased the beauty of Anatolian embroidery and the craft traditions associated with Turkish textiles. Richly embroidered dresses, jackets and coats pieced together in a patchwork of Turkish cloth and fragments of traditional folk dress gave way to the solitary long black modernist Western coat, symbolizing the loss of local sartorial identity under pressure from the global reach of Western fashion. But ending on an optimistic note, the finale saw the black dress change bit by bit back into the ethnic costume that had opened the show.

In a 2005 interview with *International Herald Tribune* Fashion Editor Suzy Menkes, Hussein Chalayan described how he was shocked to have been described as a Muslim designer but nevertheless delighted that there is a fashion designer named Hussein active in the West. He acknowledged how his work is influenced by his nonreligious Turkish roots and tempered by his later education at Central Saint Martins. 'I often have a moment of discomfort at Chalayan's shows and that is because he has the power of all creative fashion designers to capture cultural or social change, even before we are aware of it. Sometimes he seems almost prescient,' wrote Menkes in the interview.

'Those aeroplane flight paths that were used as a print in an early collection in March 1995, and the subsequent fascination with a plane's wing tips opening as flaps on dresses, seem clairvoyant in the wake of the September the 11th disaster.'

In 2004, Hussein Chalayan celebrated the 10th anniversary of his label. He earned the British Designer of the Year award in 1999 and 2000 and was made an MBE in 2006. Yet he is still true to his Turkish roots, and teaches part-time in Istanbul as well as collaborating with Turquality, an organization promoting Turkish brands.

In 2010, *Vogue* launched a Turkish edition, the first in any Western Asian country, while blogs such as Fashistanbuller mark a new era of fashion media for Turkey. But above all, since the 1990s Turkish designers, spearheaded by Hussein Chalayan, have managed to pull off the trick of transforming their uniquely Turkish sources of inspiration into modern designs, acting as agents of change in global fashion. With such a plethora of local talent, now furnished with the means to display and distribute their creations abroad, Turkey is well on its way to founding yet another empire, this time of the fashion variety.

RECOMMENDED DESIGNERS AND RESOURCES *Turkey*

Rıfat Özbek,
Dice Kayek
Hussein Chalayan
Cemil İpekçi
Yıldırım Mayruk
Arzu Karpol

Left Designer Hussein Chalayan

Opposite Model walks for Turkish Cypriot designer Hussein Chalayan Autumn/Winter 2007, Paris

A young girl prepares to wear an *Abaya* full covering dress

Gulf States: Qatar, Bahrain, Kuwait

The term 'Persian Gulf States' refers to six monarchical Arab states who since 1981 have constituted the Cooperation Council for the Arab States of the Gulf: Bahrain, Saudi Arabia, the sultanate of Oman, Kuwait, Qatar and the United Arab Emirates (UAE). From the bustling street-style scene of Kuwait City to the towering mausoleums of luxury retail lining the streets of Dubai, a region rich in natural resources such as oil and gas is also, not surprisingly, one that finds itself able to be very smartly dressed, and accordingly has fostered a surprising number of promising young couturiers as opposed to ready-to-wear designers. Experiencing a period of boom as the price of oil continues to rise as the emerging powers of China and India consume increasing volumes of oil, while economies in the West are close to bust, the Gulf States, the UAE and

Kuwait in particular have become havens of luxury and couture for Middle Eastern fashionistas.

The *khalij*, a traditional regional dress that is characteristic of Kuwait, Bahrain, Qatar and the United Arab Emirates, shares with Arab-Islamic dress in general a core underlying code, with both sexes typically covering themselves from head to toe. Many women in the region wear the *burqa* and cover their faces as well (it is mandatory in Saudi Arabia), though in the UAE Islamic dress code is not enforced.

The *thob* is the main garment for men in the Gulf, which is also known as a *dishdasha* in Kuwait or a *kandoura* in the Emirates. In Qatar, the *thob* resembles a long-sleeved, ankle-length dress shirt. The sleeves are cuffed and secured by dress buttons or cufflinks made of gold or precious stones. In both Qatar and Bahrain, the *thob* features a collar not unlike that of the Western men's dress shirt. The *ghutra*, a big, square cloth folded and placed over the top of the head, is worn in all four *khalij*-wearing societies. In the summer season, the *ghutra* is made of cotton and is bright white or sometimes a red-and-white-checked pattern. In wintertime, it is woven from soft, expensive wool in an off-white colour with long coloured lines at the ends of the cloth.

The *abaya*, a traditional Arab cloak that you don over your clothing when leaving the privacy of home has, in recent years, become the go-to garment for Islamic women seeking to uphold traditional norms whilst simultaneously wishing to express their individual style. The *abaya* is worn differently in each state: in Qatar and the Emirates, over the head with both front ends lifted and held by hand to reveal the colour and shape of the clothes worn beneath; in Kuwait and Bahrain, it is more customary to wear the *abaya* over the head, letting it fall to the ankles so as to cover the woman's clothing entirely, revealing only the face and hands. Norms in those two countries permit women

to leave their homes without wearing the *abaya*, so apparently it is entirely a woman's choice to wear it.

Today the *abaya*, instead of creating anonymity, has become a personal fashion statement, and elaborate and colourful versions abound on the runways of the Muslim world. In stores the calibre of London's landmark Harrods, luxury *abayas* have appeared in unusual silhouettes with extravagant embellishment as subtle as narrow black braid stitched along the end of the sleeve and front opening, or as exuberant as multicoloured appliqué. Embroidery has become popular along with beads and sequins, lace, ruffles, appliqué, fringe and even tassels. *Abayas* too are subject to the whim of whatever is the current trend. For example, in 2008 the craze was for *abayas* with small mandarin collars.

RECOMMENDED DESIGNERS AND RESOURCES
Saudi Arabia

Amina Al-Jassim
Adnan Akbar
Yahya Al-Bishri

Arab man sitting on patio, side profile view.

Portrait of woman walking at the beach, Dubai, UAE

Model presents a traditional *Abaya* dress at the World Costumes' Show in Doha, 2007

Linzzi Stoppard in an *Abaya* designed by Bruce Oldfield, 2008

Qatar

Until the 1950s, Qatar was the poorest of all the Arab Gulf nations, its citizens eking out a subsistence living on fishing and pearl diving, but today its sovereign wealth fund owns Harrods, the discovery and exploitation of oil and natural gas in the mid-20th century having catapulted the tiny nation into global prominence. Indeed, during the early 21st century Qatar has enjoyed the fifth highest income per capita in the world. The country is ruled by Sheikh Hamad bin Khalifa Al-Thani, a hereditary emir who is considered one of the most liberal rulers in the Arabian Gulf region. All women are encouraged to pursue education as well as employment and are allowed to drive, vote and hold public office.

A generation ago, Qatari women were robed and veiled, seldom venturing outside the family enclave. But in the early 21st century, they are pursuing higher education in ever-increasing numbers, travelling internationally, and even running their own businesses. Unlike in neighbouring Saudi Arabia, the United Arab Emirates and Iran, the Qatari law which at the start of the 21st century still requires women to cover themselves is not legally enforced. However, due to social custom, national pride and family pressure, virtually all Qatari women wear the *abaya* and the *shayla* (a scarf that functions as a head covering) within the boundaries of Qatar and when travelling to another Gulf country.

Qatar's capital, Doha, is its fashion centre. Bespoke tailors abound in Doha, catering to a clientele of many professional and upper-class women who prefer to have their *abayas* custom-made, even if it costs them thousands of dollars. Qatari women, like all wealthy women in the Gulf, accessorize their *abayas* with designer-brand accents – oversized Chanel sunglasses, perhaps, or a quilted Dior handbag. Every imaginable makeup and perfume brand is available in Qatar's modern shopping malls, and expensive handbags and shoes abound.

Qatar-based fashion brand Toujouri, now stocked at Harrods and in Dubai's ultra-trendy boutique Sauce, is the state's most successful fashion label. Launched in 2008, the brainchild of Creative Director Lama El-Moatessem, Toujouri combines traditional techniques with modern silhouettes. A graduate of the famous London College of Fashion & Central St Martins School of Fashion, after several years at the houses of Chloe and Matthew Williamson, Lama El-Moatessem founded the brand with the aim of creating luxurious garments combining the most lavish fabrics with an astute attention to detail.

Model wears a creation by Bahraini designer Shaima Al Mansoori for the Sping/Summer 2006 collection at Beirut Fashion Week

Bahrain

Top Model wears a creation by Bahraini designer Shaima Al Mansoori for the Spring/Summer 2006 collection at Beirut Fashion Week

Bahrain is a small island country of roughly a million people spread across an archipelago of 33 small islands. Like other countries in the region, it has grown wealthy over the past 50 years from exploiting its huge reserves of oil, but it also has the biggest banking sector and the freest economy in the Middle East.

Kubra Al-Qaseer is the designer largely credited with founding Bahrain's vibrant fashion scene. Her aesthetic is a combination of traditional Arabic styles with jolts of Western flamboyance – her range of revealing 'sexy *burqa*s' caused quite a stir. Kubra Al-Quaseer has a number of boutiques in Bahrain under the brand name Al Sa'fa.

Khaleda Rajab is another of the emirate's young fashion pioneers. Khaleda started designing in the mid-1990s whilst studying at the University of Suffolk in Boston. She founded her label upon returning to Bahrain, taking it upon herself to create fashions which would appeal to the masses, regardless of taste, religion or budget. In recent years, the designer has been manufacturing her own textiles and unique prints, and in 2009 her collection opened Bahrain Fashion Week.

Adeeba Al Khan, the founder of Anmar Couture, is one of Bahrain's best-loved designers, a fixture on the scene since 1999. Blending Islamic dress with detail and design elements from both East and West, Adeeba Al Khan and her colourful ranges of luxury *abayas* and *jalabiyas* have gathered a loyal following in Bahrain and beyond, with eponymous shops in both Saudi Arabia and Abu Dhabi.

Lastly, young designer Shaikha Shaima bint Abdulla Al Mansoori is one of the most promising fashion designers working in the Gulf today, with her label Mansoori Couture. A graduate of the London College of Fashion, she was selected by the Ministry of the Exterior to represent the Kingdom of Bahrain in one of the largest fashion shows in Italy amongst the world's leading fashion designers. Since then, she has shown her work at some of the most prestigious shows around the world, including Beirut Fashion Week.

RECOMMENDED DESIGNERS AND RESOURCES
Bahrain

Khaleda Rajab
http://www.khaledarajab.com
Kubra Al-Qaseer
Adeeba Al Khan

Kuwait

'Merging contemporary with traditional.'

Like nearby Bahrain, Kuwait is another small state that has grown fantastically rich on oil revenues since gaining independence from Britain in 1961. Only just over half of its roughly 3½ million people are ethnically Arab, with the significant groups of Indians, Egyptians, Syrians and Iranians living there making it one of the most ethnically diverse countries in the region.

Designer Haya Al Houti is most likely Kuwait's most successful fashion export. Since launching her label Haya Al Houti Haute Couture in 2002, she has been the only Haute Couture designer from Kuwait to have participated in the Couture Fashion Week in New York in 2007.

Kuwait, in addition to a thriving local couture industry, also has the most developed and active fashion blogosphere and gaggle of e-zines of all the Gulf States. The blog Confashions from Kuwait has published over 1400 articles since its launch in 2007 and has amassed a strong following. Visual diary/street style blog beICONq8, the brainchild of Maha Al Wanyan (photographer and editor), Naif Al Thuwaini (graphic designer) and Yousef Al Taher (model), chronicles Kuwait's underground hipster scene and the rich street style that is rife in Kuwait.

Khaleejesque is a Kuwaiti-based online lifestyle magazine that covers all things hip in the Arabian Gulf countries. 'This is a modern girl's guide to cultural dressing,' reads a description on the website. 'Merging contemporary with traditional. It's how we envision the Khaleejesque girl to dress. Embracing culture, but adding her own unique touches.'

RECOMMENDED DESIGNERS AND RESOURCES *Kuwait*

Haya Al Houti, Confashion from Kuwait – Blog http://www. confashionsfromkuwait.com

A model displays a creation by Kuwaiti fashion designer Haya Al-Houti at her Summer 2009 Haute Couture collection, Beirut

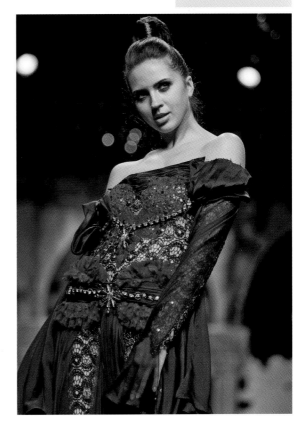

A model displays a creation by Kuwaiti fashion designer Haya Al-Houti at her Summer 2009 Haute Couture collection, Beirut

UAE Emirati women dressed in the traditional *abaya*

UAE: Dubai & Abu Dhabi

'Every culture has its traditions and you have to respect this while giving it a twist.'

The United Arab Emirates (UAE) is a federation of seven states situated in the southeast of the Persian Gulf, bordering Oman and Saudi Arabia and consisting of the emirates of Abu Dhabi, Dubai, Sharjah, Ajman, Umm al-Quwain, Ras al-Khaimah and Fujairah. With the world's seventh-largest oil reserves, the UAE – Dubai and Abu Dhabi in particular–have enjoyed a long period of economic prosperity, making the region one of the global fashion industry's most important emerging markets.

Unlike neighbouring Saudi Arabia, where *niqabs* still dominate and limit women's wardrobes, the Islamic dress code is not compulsory in the UAE, though most Emirati women still wear the *abaya*. However, the *abaya* has lent itself to the Arab designer as the traditional silhouette which preserves traditional values but nevertheless allows for some form of individual sartorial expression. The UAE, being less conservative and more cosmopolitan than some of its Islamic neighbours, has become the incubator for the reinvention of the *abaya* for the couturier and the catwalk, the fundamental ingredients of an emerging cultural identity for a new breed of fashion designers from the Arab world.

'"There is no contradiction between the modernity of European fashion and [the] modernity of Middle Eastern women,"' Tamara Hostal, Director of Esmod Dubai (the internationally acclaimed French fashion institution which set up a school in the emirate to encourage its young fashion talent), told Bloomberg in 2010. '"Every culture has its traditions and you have to respect this while giving it a twist."'

Models dressed in contemporary *abayas* designed by international designers in Paris, 2009

Dubai

Dubbed the 'shopping capital of the Middle East,' Dubai, with its 70-plus malls and the bustling marketplaces of its famous souk districts, is the tax-free fashion haven of the UAE. Its big spenders are legendary, their extravagance unmatched at a time when much of the Western world suffers from the pinch of the global recession. Riding high on the tailcoat of Dubai's oil-fuelled real-estate boom during the period bookended by the two Gulf Wars (from 1990 to 2004, Dubai's gross domestic product quadrupled to $27 billion, according to the Dubai Department of Economic Development), fashion of the most decadent and luxurious kind found its new Babylon.

Major Western brands rushed to set up extravagant boutiques to cater to a luxury-hungry clientele of wealthy emirate women and tourists who poured in from abroad. Giorgio Armani, the first designer with the prescience to set up shop in Dubai in the mid-1990s in the wake of the Gulf War, has since opened the doors to an ultra-lavish Armani Hotel in the emirate's Burj Khalifa, the world's tallest building, in 2010. In 2006, Christian Dior had one store in the Middle East – in Dubai. Since then, the French house has opened outposts in Saudi Arabia, Qatar, Bahrain, Lebanon, Kuwait and elsewhere in the UAE. Today, one would be hard-pressed to name a luxury label not easily accessible in Dubai's tax-free boutiques and department stores.

In addition to a traditional fashion week (Dubai Fashion Week was launched in 2006), the emirate also plays host a massive retail event, the Dubai Shopping Festival, which was launched in 1996 to revitalize the flagging retail industry after the war. The event has since evolved into an international tourist affair of epic proportions, attracting some 35 million visitors since its inception. In 2009 alone, visitors surpassed the 3.35 million mark and spent Dh9.8 billion during the month-long event. Dubai's nickname, the 'City of Gold' was coined during one of the Shopping Festival's early awareness campaigns.

As for the local design scene, such wealth and focus on luxury has spawned a generation of talented young couturiers. Sheikh Khalid Bin Sultan Al Qasimi, born into the Emirate royal family and founder of the Qasimi couture label, is perhaps the best-known internationally. Now based in London, Khalid first showed at London Fashion Week during the Autumn/Winter 2008 season. His show for the following autumn (Autumn/Winter 2009) was something of a coup as the presentation boasted an all-star line-up of supermodels. Lily Cole, Yasmin Le Bon, Jade Parfitt and Carmen Dell'Orefice all walked tall in exquisite Victorian-style black corseted silk evening gowns styled with elaborate millinery. For Spring/Summer 2010, Khalid adopted a luxurious Arabic theme and his collection was wrought with heavily embellished separates in metallic gold and rich red inspired by the Gulf's *jalabiyas*. In 2010, Khalid took a season off from the women's ready-to-wear scene and launched a menswear line in Paris after an invitation from Didier Grumbach, the President of the Fédération Française de la Couture, du Prêt à Porter des Couturiers et des Créateurs de Mode (aka the Chambre Syndicale), one of the most important figures in the fashion industry. As Khalid told UAE news website thenational.ae in February 2010, "'Although it was all a bit last-minute, Monsieur Grumbach said there was room for me to do an

> ## 'I know what men want to wear.'

installation in Paris and I jumped at the chance. Menswear comes so naturally to me. I know what men want to wear.'"

Furne One is another successful designer who has managed to build a successful couture house in Dubai. Born in the Philippines, One is representative of the emirate's large ex-patriot community, and his designs are an amalgam of his Eastern background, his decade-long sojourn in Dubai, and his frequent European travels. "'[Dubai's] a melting pot of races; in fact, there are more expats there than locals – lots of Europeans. It's also an open city; not as strict as other Arabic cities,'" One told the *Asian Journal* in 2009 after being invited to show at Miami Fashion Week.

In 2008, Furne One shot to fame in Germany after Heidi Klum enlisted him to design the gowns for all 18 models in the final round of Germany's Next Top Model. Following the show, Furne One was invited to present at Berlin Fashion Week in January 2009. For Autumn/Winter 2010, Furne One's collection for his label Amato Haute Couture at Dubai Fashion Week consisted of intricately hand-beaded corseted

Models pose in designer *abayas* by Emirati designer Lamia Abdin

Model dressed in a contemporary *abaya*

and caged dresses in soft creams overlaid with glittering chainmail – inspired by King Arthur.

The label DAS (an initialism for Daffa, Abba and Suwaieya, referring to the different styles of traditional *abayas* that are worn across the Gulf region), launched in 2008 by two Emirati sisters, is a range of luxury *abayas* for the 21st-century Islamic woman. Designer sisters Reem and Hind Beljafla use colour, embroidery and even metal studs to add a dash of fashion flair to the traditionally plain, all-black garments. In addition to their flagship store in Dubai, London's Harrods started selling *abayas* from the DAS Collection in the summer of 2010, just one month after Qatar's sovereign-wealth fund bought the famous Knightsbridge store. The sisters count members of the UAE's royal family and that of Oman amongst their devoted fans, some of whom have even requested the pair to make *abayas* to match their Birkin bags and Gucci shoes, "'because they will be wearing the *abaya* in public where they cannot show a dress that would match with their accessories,'" as Beljafla told Bloomberg in a 2010 interview. An *abaya* from DAS can cost up to $5000.

In the autumn of 2008 Dubai's property bubble collapsed, but its shockwaves have yet to be seriously felt across its fashion sector, as can be seen in the continued growth of Dubai Fashion Week. Under new ownership in 2010, the fashion week is looking to solidify its position as an industry leader within the region – and this means a concerted effort in shifting the focus away from its international inspirations to focus on local, Dubai-based designers. As Saif Ali Khan, Vice President, Dubai Fashion Week is quoted as saying on notjustalabel.com (a global business directory for showcasing avant-garde designers), "'The Emerging Talent Segment, the highlight of the Dubai Fashion Week, will gain more prominence this year. It has been very successful over the years and we would like to offer similar opportunities to every budding designer from the region and beyond.'"

Indeed, the youth of Dubai are thirsting for a platform for creative expression, as catwalk designers such as DAS focus primarily on the reinterpretation of the *abaya* for an elite female clientele, disregarding the youth zeitgeist and street-style trends. 'Young adults have developed their own style of expressing themselves,' blogged Nia Beazer on her cult site Dubai's It Girl in 2010, 'and it is truly reminiscent of different Hip Hop era gear, integrated with Arabic influences. I wish someone would take notice of the urban street style in this country and make something for our youth.'

Abu Dhabi

'The fashion week is the first step to make a statement within the region that the city of Abu Dhabi supports Arabic value and creativity.'

Abu Dhabi is the capital of and the second largest city in the United Arab Emirates. Home to the important offices of the federal government, it is also the seat for the United Arab Emirates Government. Accordingly, in recent years, Abu Dhabi has blossomed into a cosmopolitan cultural capital, particularly in the field of contemporary art. In 2009 the launch of Abu Dhabi Art, an international multi-venue event described as 'an arts platform', revealed the emirate's aspirations to establish itself as a major cultural destination.

Abu Dhabi launched its first fashion week in March 2008 to much media fanfare as the event closed with a sensational presentation of Valentino's haute-couture collection. The success of its debut event, followed by a second later the same year, suggested that Abu Dhabi Fashion Week is emerging as the premier high-profile fashion industry event in the Middle East. 'We started Abu Dhabi Fashion Week as part of a wider initiative linked with the fashion industry,' stated Dr Alice Teeuwen, chairperson of Maven Corporate, the event's organizer, in its official press release. 'We're happy that Abu Dhabi Fashion Week has evolved into a successful business-driven event that focuses on showcasing international designers seeking greater exposure to the rapidly growing consumers'

markets of the Middle East, South Asia and Africa, and on providing a platform and infrastructure for leading local and regional designers to reach out to the international fashion markets.'

Aisha bin Desmal is Abu Dhabi's best-known designer and her Autumn/Winter 2008 collection opened the inaugural Abu Dhabi Fashion Week. Like DAS, Desmal's label focuses on the reinterpretation of the *abaya* alongside innovations in traditional wedding and engagement clothes.

An initiative called She Arabia was launched alongside Abu Dhabi Fashion Week, showcasing the work of ten Emirati students from the Sheikh Zayed Private Academy. It met with such great success that She Arabia became a brand and is now an integral part of the event.

'"The inclusion of these students in the event is in conformity with our vision to develop fashion designing in the country and to encourage and provide avenues for our talented designers to evolve into international creators,"' Mr Ali Al Badi, Director of Abu Dhabi's Fashion Resources Park, pointed out to ameinfo.com. '"What we want to create is a centre of excellence, by bringing a lot of elements together. And the fashion week is the first step to make a statement within the region that the city of Abu Dhabi supports Arabic value and creativity."'

RECOMMENDED DESIGNERS AND RESOURCES *UAE*

Sheikh Khalid Bin Sultan Al Qasimi
Aisha Bin Desmal
Furne One
DAS http://www. dascollection.com
Dubai Fashion Week http:// www.dfw.ae

Creation by Emirati designer Aisha bin Desmal at Abu Dhabi Fashion Week 2008

Models present creations by designers from the Sheikh Zayed Private Academy at Abu Dhabi Fashion Week, 2008

asia

Introduction

Of all the world's cultures, none have romanced the Western artistic and sartorial imaginations quite like those of the Far East. From the flowing kimonos of Japan, to the high-collared *cheongsams* of China and the voluminous saris of India, the reach of East Asia's sartorial influence is as vast and diverse as the region itself. Dating back as far as ancient Rome and coming to fruition in the 19th century with the opening of Asia to the West, the Occident has long been enchanted by the exoticism of the Orient and the luxury it has come to represent. From Chanel to Prada to Vivienne Westwood, there is hardly an established Western designer who has not, at some point in their career, drawn from that well of inspiration. And as the engine of the global economy shifts ever further eastward, many of the major Western brands are beginning to realize that not only should they be looking to the Orient for inspiration, but they should also be designing specifically for and catering to a hungry, emerging fashion market.

'I would hate myself for having made something so easy to understand.'

More so than Africa, the Middle East or Latin America, Eastern Asia's contribution to global fashion lies in shape, cut and silhouette. Of course, fabrics, embroidery and beading techniques also play a part in defining Asian sartorial style, but it is in the attention to cut in traditional dress, from Korean *hanbok* to the *baro't saya* of the Philippines, that the most significant contribution to the runways of the West can be seen. Traditional Asian dress depends on an awareness of lines and methods of construction, whereas contemporary Asian design focuses on deconstruction and experimentation with boundaries,– in other words, the design is often quite cerebral. Japanese designer Rei Kawakubo of Comme des Garçons, for example, always seeks to reveal the complexity within simplicity in her work. "'Suppose everyone likes my collection and says, 'the show was great' and 'the clothes were beautiful', then I become very uneasy. I would hate myself for having made something so easy to understand,'" Kawakubo remarked in 2005 to Sanae Shimizu.

Opposite A design by Rei Kawakubo displayed at the 'Blog.mode: addressing fashion' exhibit at the Metropolitan Museum of Art's Costume Institute, 2007

Yohji Yamamoto
Autumn/Winter
2009, Paris

Yohji Yamamoto
Autumn/Winter
2006, Paris

Model displays a beads embroidered peacock dress with a large floating shawl at Hanae Mori's 2003 Autumn/Winter Haute Couture collection in Tokyo

Anna Sui Spring/Summer 2009, New York

'Thai people love fashion.'

Inspiration and cross-cultural exchange goes both ways, of course, and generations of young talents in the West have re-imagined traditional Asian dress often to a startling effect. The best example of this is perhaps British designer Zandra Rhodes's reinterpretation of the sari. This 1987 show became such an iconic example of contemporary Indian design that not only did it inspire a new generation of Indian fashion designers, it was also chosen by the SEIBU stores in Tokyo to represent India itself in the first Festival of India in Japan. Thanks, in part, to Zandra Rhodes's foreign eye breathing new life into the centuries-old garment which is such an integral part of Indian daily life, India today has one of the most exciting fashion scenes on this vast continent, with a host of institutes ready to educate an eager generation of fashion hopefuls.

In the harmonious manner of yin and yang, this symbiotic relationship between Eastern and Western fashions and fashion designers has fostered a thriving Asian sartorial culture, both at home and abroad, as well as spawning one of the world's most fascinating and dynamic street-style scenes. The Asian love of fashion and hunger for big brands is paramount in driving commerce, making the region especially appealing for Western brands, as Thai designer Koi Suwannagate remarks. "Thai people love fashion. They are huge fans of the big names and anything that relates to celebrity culture." Japanese street style is regarded as the best in the world, with subcultures such as Gothic Lolita having gained enough momentum to be classified as cultural movements in their own right.

Southeast Asia probably lags behind its Chinese and Japanese counterparts in terms of key exports on the international scene and also in the support they give

Chinese models displays dresses designed with motifs of the
Forbidden City and its treasure by Hu Xiaodan, Tokyo, 2006

Model wears Chinese inspired headdress for
Jean Paul Gaultier Autumn/Winter 2010, Paris

their young designers. Thanks in part to a burgeoning blogosphere, however, the region has in recent years seen an explosion of young talent, both in design and in other creative facets of the fashion industry, such as photography. Filipino blogger Bryan Grey-Yambao of cult site BryanBoy started blogging at the age of 17 from his parents' home in Manila. Hanifa Ambadar, founder of Fashionese Daily, Indonesia's premier fashion blog, is adamant in her belief that the internet and other new technologies will be the vehicle through which local talent can reach a bigger audience. "Indonesian indie designers are definitely a force we can't leave behind as they already have such a huge following. Since they are young, they use technology in their day-to-day life, so it helps them in promoting their designs. They have used Twitter, Facebook, websites and other [digital] media to gain followers." The same holds true for Korea. "Twitter, Facebook, fashion blogs – through things like these, people can access the new collection as

soon as it comes out, almost simultaneously, thus the influence which only a few fashion editors used to have is no longer only theirs anymore," comments Korean designer Lie Sang Bong.

With fashion gaining so much momentum in Eastern Asia, and the emergence of a regional fashion industry, designed, produced, marketed and sold locally, the region is potentially poised to break away from the Eurocentric sartorial traditions of Paris, Milan and London. Soon a new generation of Japanese designers will want to set up their ateliers in Tokyo rather than following in the footsteps of pioneers Yohji Yamamoto and Issey Miyake, for instance, and relocating to Paris. Soon, too, perhaps Western designers will be clamouring for space on the runways of Shanghai and Jakarta instead of New York and Paris, signalling the beginning of a new chapter in the global fashion story, one with an Eastern epicentre.

Model walks the runway at the Digital Clutch Design reveal by HP and Vivienne Tam, New York, 2009

China

There's no denying that China is well on its way to becoming one of the world's superpowers of the future. Home to over 1.3 billion people, the People's Republic of China contains around 20% of the entire global human population. However, despite the might of their numbers and their dazzlingly rich sartorial history, stretching back some 5,000 years, the Chinese fifth of the world's numbers does not translate to an equivalent influence on the fashion world. Up until very recently, China's contribution to global fashion has often been at the level of production (albeit on a massive scale), proverbially summed up by familiar words 'made in China' stitched onto the labels of many of the garments bought by Western consumers.

This is not to say that traditional ethnic Chinese dress as well as Chinese designers themselves have not influenced the catwalks of the West: Karl Lagerfeld, Giorgio Armani and Dries van Noten,

for example, have all claimed the *qipao* or *cheongsam* (known colloquially in the West as the 'Suzie Wong' dress after the 1960 film *The World of Suzie Wong*, starring Nancy Kwan) as inspiration for some of their runway looks over the years. And Cantonese-born designer Vivienne Tam's creations, with their signature East-meets-West aesthetic, have continued to impress on the runways of New York since 1994.

Supermodel Liu Wen, born in Hunan Province, is an omnipresent willowy fixture on the catwalks of the major fashion houses, often the face of their international campaigns, as is her compatriot Du Juan. And for the launch of his latest Métier D'Arts Collection in 2010, Karl Lagerfeld, inspired by an imaginary voyage to Shanghai by Mademoiselle Coco Chanel, created a Chanel interpretation of the Paris–Shanghai journey, drawing upon the romanticism of 1930s Shanghai.

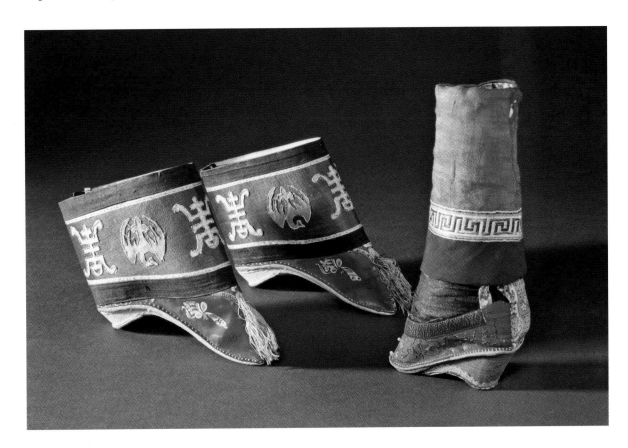

Wooden soled shoes for women with bound feet, c.1870–1910

Chinese-American actress Anna May Wong on set c.1935

Woman modelling a Chinese dress with embroidered flowers on the sleeves and collar, 1949

China's relationship with dress, with fashion, is much more complex than can be summed up by a brief who's who of the country's most renowned fashion exports. More so than most nations, China's fashion history, like the history of the country itself, is inextricably bound up in its politics and its shifting ideology.

Traditional Chinese clothing is broadly referred to as *hanfu*, and the most common of its garments throughout history was some form of coat or robe. Though the basic shape underwent many manifestations for which the Chinese had an equal variety of names, one of the most common was the *yi*, which resembled a Japanese-style kimono. Cinched with a *tao*, or sash, the *yi* was worn over an ankle-length skirt called the *chang*. There was also the *shenyi* or 'deep robe', which trailed behind the wearer and featured long sleeves covering the arms and hands – the typical picture of Chinese male attire in the West. *Hanfu* typically conforms to the social mores as laid down by Confucianism. That is to say, one's fashion choices would be strictly defined by one's status in society. Han society was an ordered one, and this order–from the Emperor down to the most unregarded peasant–was clearly visible in dress. Accordingly, changes in power were always

accompanied by changes in fashion – literally, the Emperor's new clothes – from one generation to the next. While all manner of dress across all walks of Chinese society was obliged to evolve as a new dynasty succeeded the previous one, it was not until the last chapter in the country's dynastic saga, the Qing Dynasty that ruled from 1644 to 1911, that major cultural and sartorial reform took place. This began with the two Opium Wars fought between the British and the Chinese on the Chinese mainland. The first of these was concluded in 1842 by the signing of the Treaty of Nanjing, in which the Chinese were forced to open four treaty ports to the West and to cede Hong Kong to Britain. Within 20 years, popular Western fashions such as jacquard fabrics, silk trimmings, laces, fancy braids and gilt or enamelled buttons, were freely entering China.

The collapse of the Qing dynasty and the establishment of the Republic of China in 1912 brought sweeping social changes for women, which were quickly reflected in a new order of dress for the modern liberated woman. Foot binding was legally abolished and women embraced silk stockings and heeled shoes. Dress styles became shorter, revealing ankles, and Western-style undergarments came into vogue to flatter the more form-fitting shapes. Trend-conscious young girls began to don hybridized Han, Manchu and Western dress, including the *magua*, a short front-fastening jacket, with trousers and Western accessories. Department stores carried ready-to-wear clothes of all types, their windows proudly displaying copies of the latest high fashions from Europe.

The now-Western-infused sensibilities of the local population, combined with a growing sense of how Eastern exoticism enhanced the European aesthetic, led to the creation of the *cheongsam*, a form-fitting dress with a high Mandarin collar developed in 1920s Shanghai, which by then had earned the chic nickname 'Paris of the East'. The silhouette became wildly popular and various versions abounded, including floor-length dresses for eveningwear and knee-length ones for daywear. Dressmakers experimented with new materials, including artificial silk and geometric patterns on trend with the art deco fashions that were so popular in Europe at the time. However, the use of Chinese-only materials (as decreed by the new government) reflected a rising sense of Chinese nationalism.

Following the Chinese Civil War in the late 1940s, which saw the Communist Party headed by Mao Zedong assume control of the newly proclaimed People's Republic of China (PRC), garments thought to reflect either traditional values or modern Western fashions were branded reactionary. Proletarian revolutionary styles that were in tune with promoted national ideals, such as frugality, austerity and egalitarianism, quickly became popular.

Models wear a re-creation of court robes for an Emperor and Empress in the Qing Dynasty of China

Red dress with a Mao collar by Shanghai Tang, Hong Kong Fashion Week 2009

The launch of economic reforms in 1978 stimulated social and cultural change, which had far-reaching effects on contemporary fashion. While 'resistance to bourgeois liberation' remained high up on the official political agenda, Western influence began to seep into all walks of Chinese society. Controversial Western styles such as bell-bottom trousers, flowery shirts, jeans, sunglasses and high heels were typical of avant-garde fashion during the transitional period at the end of the 1970s and early 1980s. China's first fashion magazine, *Shizhuang*, was launched in 1980, and a slew of others followed straight after. In 1988, *Elle* began to publish in Shanghai and over the next two decades 20 years, Chinese-language editions of leading international fashion magazines (*Vogue*, *Harper's Bazaar*, *Cosmopolitan*, *Marie Claire* and *Seventeen*) have become ubiquitous on China's news stands.

Though 1979 witnessed China's first runway show (the government invited French designer Pierre Cardin to present his collections in Beijing and Shanghai), the major influences on Chinese fashion at that time came from Hong Kong and via Hong Kong from Taiwan through manufacturing. Hong Kong's position as a manufacturing base for Levi jeans and other designer-label merchandise made it the major exporter of international fashion in the 1970s, but by the mid-1990s the number one garment producer and exporter was China. International luxury brands such as Chanel, Dior, Louis Vuitton and Armani, now established in China, were highly sought-after by the country's nouveau riche. Domestic fashion designers subsequently established labels and businesses that were and still continue to be marketed across China and internationally. In 1994, Hong Kong entrepreneur and nightclub owner David Tang founded Shanghai Tang, China's first real brand.

Meanwhile abroad, Chinese ethnic dress captivated the imaginations of some of Europe's most

Top Portrait of a young Mao Zedong wearing the Mao cap, 1925

Right Shanghai Tang, Hong Kong Luxury Week 2009

John Galliano for Christian Dior Haute Couture Spring/Summer 2008, Paris

Shoes form John Galliano Spring/Summer 2009, Paris

compelling designers: Yves Saint Laurent drew influence from Chinese dress closures and Manchu dragon-robe patterns in his 1977 collections, and Christian Lacroix tried his hand at the complicated embroidered patchwork *cheongsam* in his Autumn/Winter 1992 collection. With influences to offer ranging from the splendour of the printed silks of imperial court dress, to the conical sunshade straw hats worn by peasants toiling in the fields, to traditional military armour, once China's ports were opened to the West, the exchange of culture flowed both ways, from Europe into Hong Kong and from mainland China via Hong Kong into the Western world. "'It was 1979 when I went with one of the first groups of Americans to China when China was opened up,'" recounts British designer Zandra Rhodes. "'I then did a wonderful Chinese collection with exotic Chinese-inspired hats, pagoda sleeves and garments in lacquer reds and olive-green colourways.'"

The *cheongsam*, the dress synonymous with the traditional Chinese woman and symbolic of the somewhat erotic exoticism from which the silhouette was born, is without a doubt the most imitated shape on European runways. In 1997, the year British designer John Galliano took over creative direction at Christian Dior, the designer slyly referenced another handover – that of Britain returning sovereignty of Hong Kong to China – by reworking the *cheongsam* at his first haute couture show in Paris. A few years earlier New York-based, American-born Chinese designer Anna Sui had shown a collection of *cheongsams* using *devoré* velvet, with mandarin collars, for Spring/Summer 1993, while Chinese Malaysian-born designer Yeohlee Teng (based in the United States and known as Yeolhee) refers frequently to the *cheongsam* and other forms of Chinese ethnic dress in her designs, most notably the mandarin-collared creations from her Autumn/Winter 1996 show.

Model in
an outfit by
Karl Lagerfeld at
Chanel's Paris
Shanghai fashion
show 2009,
Shanghai

Louis Vuitton
Spring/Summer
2011, Paris

Anna Sui Spring/Summer 2009, New York

Vivienne Tam Spring/Summer 2010, New York

But perhaps the *cheongsam's* most famous turn along the catwalk came in the form of the mandarin collars that featured in both of Prada's collections for 1997, bearing a silk willow-leaf print that was reversed and shown in a number of colours, which were then widely copied on the Western high street. Miuccia Prada, for her second line Miu Miu that same year, showed a pie-crust frill at a *cheongsam* neckline worn open, a sartorial gesture that in Hong Kong identifies the wearer to be a prostitute. Hong Kong designers Walter Ma and Peter Lau have used the shape as an inspiration, notably in the latter's 1997 Liberty print version, which was a visual realization of the East/West dynamic. Another Hong Kong designer, William Tang,

> '*For decades, the Hong Kong garment and textile industry has attracted buyers from all over the world because of its outstanding manufacturing craftsmanship.*'

has alluded to the *cheongsam* in his collections by restyling its basic elements–the side slits, for example–and recombining them with other fashion dress techniques.

Along with exporting the aesthetics of Chinese dress, the Chinese diaspora, specifically that in the US, has produced a healthy crop of American-born fashion industry leaders. The name Vera Wang is practically synonymous with luxury bridal wear, while Chinese merchant Ellery J. Chun invented the quintessential item of the American holiday-goer–the Aloha shirt– whilst living in Hawaii in the 1930s, and making shirts for tourists out of old kimono fabrics. Young talents Derek Lam, Peter Som, Alexander Wang and Jason Wu nip at the heels of the older generation of Chinese–American designers, people like Vivienne Tam and Anna Sui, demonstrating that the flame of Chinese fashion design in the West is only growing stronger with the passage of time.

Top left Vera Wang Autumn/Winter 2010, New York

Top right Designer Vera Wang

Bottom Vera Wang Autumn/Winter 2010, New York

Louis Vuitton Spring/Summer 2011, Paris

Louis Vuitton Spring/Summer 2011, Paris

Jean Paul Gaultier Autumn/Winter 2010, Paris

Back home, things are also changing. As we creep further and further into the 21st century and China anticipates its move towards the centre stage of global politics and economics true to its roots, wherein the path of both nation and nation's wardrobe proceed hand in hand, it is also looking to evolve its standing on the international fashion stage. Rapid economic growth has brought about increased purchasing power among the growing Chinese middle class, and as far back as the 1980s, China's export-oriented garment industry has wanted to focus on looking inward. Already saturated with European brands, government-owned organizations began to design and create new fashions and fashion-forward brands for the domestic Chinese market, attempting to focus on production quality rather than quantity.

'"For decades, the Hong Kong garment and textile industry has attracted buyers from all over the world because of its outstanding manufacturing craftsmanship and flexible trade and sales services. Hong Kong fashion designers are trendsetters who understand the market. The ultimate advantage of Hong Kong is its ability to reach the massive market on the Chinese mainland,"' comments Vincent Fang in a press release for Hong Kong Fashion Week, Chairman of the Hong Kong Trade Development Council's garment advisory committee, the organization behind Hong Kong Fashion Week.

Put more simply, over the coming years, as the fiscal and fashion epicentre of the world shifts eastward,

Jean Paul Gaultier Autumn/Winter 2010, Paris

Jean Paul Gaultier Autumn/Winter 2010, Paris

Chinese models displays dresses designed with motifs of the Forbidden City and its treasure by Hu Xiaodan, Tokyo, 2006

the fashion weeks of Beijing, Shanghai and Hong Kong may unseat the likes of London, Paris and Milan. Young domestic Chinese designers, such as Qiu Hao, who is widely regarded as one of China's most influential and avant-garde emerging fashion designers, and Hu Xiaodan, the world-famous costume designer who, looking to the drama of traditional Chinese architecture, famously created an elaborate collection paying homage to the Forbidden City, are proof of the depth and richness of talent in this vast country.

Soon the familiar words 'made in China' will start to disappear from our Nike trainers and Gap t-shirts, and the words 'designed in China' will instead grace a new era of the world's luxury brands.

RECOMMENDED DESIGNERS AND RESOURCES *China*

Vivienne Tam
Yeohlee Teng
Derek Lam
Peter Som
Alexander Wang

Jason Wu (Taiwan)
Qin Hao
Hu Xiaodan
Walter Ma
Peter Lau
William Tang

Hanae Mori
Haute Couture
'East meets
West' show,
Autumn/Winter
2004

Japan

Be it in the form of slight nuance, such as a gesture towards the geta sandal at Marc Jacobs, or the broader lending of a timeless silhouette like the kimono, the Land of the Rising Sun has arguably had more influence on European fashion design than any other Asian nation.

Secluded from the West for most of its 2000-year history, it wasn't until 1854 that Japan was opened to the outside world, and only then under threat of force by the US Navy. This 'coming out' happened to coincide with one of the most dynamic and important periods in fashion history – namely, the birth of contemporary fashion design as we know it–and Japanese culture would exert a profound influence on European artistic thinking over the next few decades, a phenomenon known as Japonism.

Ukiyo-e, a form of woodblock printing often featuring robe-clad women striking flirtatious and evocative poses, was extremely popular amongst artists at this time. And whilst its alternative sense of space and form were the qualities that captivated and inspired the likes of painters Claude Monet and James Tissot, the multilayered, long, lavish *kosode* robes worn by the women in their paintings were took the Western fashion capital by storm. In Paris, women were soon clamouring for imported *kosode* robes to wear at home. The trend soon evolved and women began deconstructing the robes and retailoring them into bustle-style silk dressing gowns or coats to be sported during a night on the town.

It is precisely this feeling of interaction, of playing with what it means to dress, and even simply to be – either 'Western' or 'Eastern' – to deconstruct and reinvent that which is familiar and that which is not; these conundrums have underpinned fashion's love affair with Japan. It is not Japan itself, but that dynamic conversation, begun in the 19th century

Great Wave of Kanagawa by Katsushika Hokusai c.1900

Ukiyo-e, Japanese woodblock print c.1861

Emperor Hirohito of Japan wearing ceremonial robes c.1920

A Japanese woman at her toilette wearing a kimono c.1940

with designers such as Paul Poiret, and carried on in the postwar era by people like Christian Dior and Yves Saint Laurent, which still continues to stalk runways around the world today.

The 45-year reign of the Meiji Emperor (1868–1912), known as the Meiji Period, launched an aggressive Westernization and modernization agenda, including the introduction of European-style suit dressing to Japanese society. After a long tradition of wearing kimonos, Japanese gents suddenly found themselves urged by the Meiji government to wear Western-style suits, often topped off with canes and bowler hats. They were followed by a small group of aristocratic women in the late 1880s, cheered on by their empress, who had already taken to donning Parisian fashions such as trendy corsets and skirts.

But luxury is usually the preserve of the rich, and 19th-century Japan was no exception. Exorbitant

price tags from Paris prevented most Japanese women from westernizing their style from head to toe. So, ever the coy and thrifty street stylists, a Japanese girl looking to give her look a modern twist did what any trend setter would do: she accessorized. A lacy, high-collar blouse could be worn under a kimono, while French satin high-heeled shoes could be paired with silk stockings instead of the traditional combination of *zori* (sandals) and *tabi* (socks). Given that jewellery, with the exception of hair ornaments, was never a part of traditional Japanese dress culture, a girl could easily update her look by pinning on a brooch or slipping on a ring. With the introduction of Western-style sewing machines in the late 1890s brought DIY European style to the masses, women in two-piece ensembles (tops and skirts) as opposed to the traditional one-piece kimono were soon ubiquitous.

By the 1910s, Japanese department stores like Takashimaya had begun selling ready-to-wear

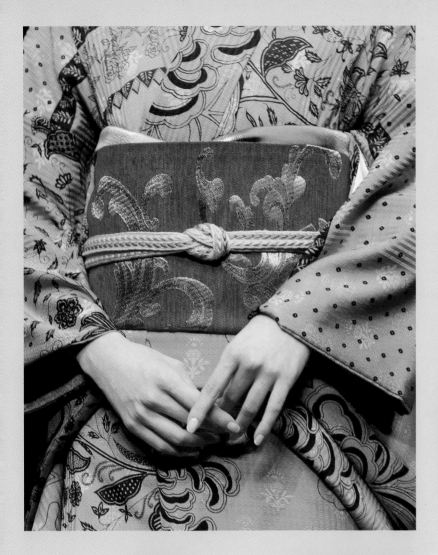

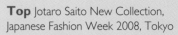

Top Jotaro Saito New Collection,
Japanese Fashion Week 2008, Tokyo

Bottom left Jotaro Saito New Collection,
Japanese Fashion Week 2008, Tokyo

Bottom right Shoes from Kenzo
Spring/Summer 2011, Paris

Model wears a creation by Naoki Takizawa for Issey Miyake Spring/Summer 2007, Paris

Western-style clothes for both men and women – the same styles gracing shop floors in London, Paris and New York. But, in a move which very much reflects that now characteristic sense of fusion in Japanese style, Tokyo's stores offered Western fashions with a Japanese twist: a modern-style kimono with funky new designs, such as skyscrapers and art deco tulips, referencing contemporaneous art movements. Soon this style of kimono, known as the taish-modo, was all the rage with women in Paris. Japan had officially arrived on the global fashion scene.

The arrival of the kimono on the early 20th-century Parisian fashion scene coincided with and arguably spurred on this major period of change in the city's ateliers. Though the kimono had influenced

Parisian fashions before, only its motifs and silk fabrics had been used, and not the actual silhouette itself. But with designers flocking to liberate clients from their corsets and crinolines, the kimono shape became a foundational point of reference for the creation of the new straight-line style of dress. The first designer actually to take this up was Coco Chanel's rival, Paul Poiret (1879–1944), whose nape-exposing, cocoon coat style of the 1920s, worn loosely around the shoulders and held closed in front with one hand, clearly drew its inspiration from Ukiyo-e.

Paul Poiret's designs were a smash hit and, from the 1880s to the 1930s, straight-line cut constructions soon came to dominate women's fashion in the West. '"Next to Poiret,"' quipped Parisian fashion designer Azzedine Alaïa, "'Coco Chanel looks like a little dressmaker'", as cited in an article in 2007 in *Dvisible Magazine* (www.dvisible.com)

Poiret was not alone in his crusade to bring Japanese aesthetics into the ateliers and onto the shop floors of Paris. Madeleine Vionnet (1876–1975), transformed the kimono's shape with a simple green silk dress in around 1925. The dress, draping freely over the body and hanging off the shoulders, featured pin-tucks that were meant to represent the raked gravel of Japanese Zen gardens. Her loose, draping aesthetic, a style which essentially we now refer to as 'Grecian', has influenced scores of designers over the decades. The label is currently designed by Rodolfo Paglialunga.

There was also Spanish couturier Mariano Fortuny (1871–1949), whose *kosode*-style coats and gowns of the 1910s, with their thick padded hems, known as fuki, and pattern-stencilled motifs, also drew obvious inspiration from Japanese textiles.

The period immediately following the Second World War saw yet another huge influx of Western culture into Japan as the country was occupied by the Allied Forces for seven years (1945–52). With occupation came elements from American popular culture, including Hollywood movies, rock 'n' roll and, of course, the introduction of casual dressing – jeans and t-shirts, etc. Simultaneously, as had happened at the turn of the century, in the late 1950s and 1960s European fashion itself was undergoing yet another revolution: the birth of ready-to-wear.

Creation by Italian designer Antonia Marras for Kenzo Autumn/Winter 2008, Paris

Creation by Dai Fujiwara for Issey Miyake Spring/Summer 2008, Paris

Yohji Yamamoto Spring/Summer 2006, Paris

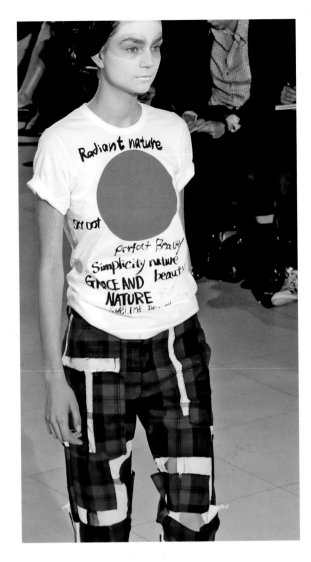

Model wears tshirt inspired by the Japanese flag at Rei Kawakubo for Comme des Garcons Spring/Summer 2007, Paris

In terms of design at home, Japanese fashion designers had to 'make it' in Paris, before their work was accepted by their peers. Kenzo Takada worked in Paris for the first decade of his career, the 1960s, before returning to Tokyo. After first showing on the catwalks in New York in 1971, and Paris in 1973, Issey Miyake then returned to Tokyo. Yohji Yamamoto also made his debut Paris in the 1980s before returning to Japan. All three designers, though often clearly drawing on their native culture in their work, still show at Paris Fashion Week today alongside fellow countrymen Junya Watanabe and Rei Kawakubo of Comme des Garçons. The underlying Japanese aesthetic of these designers stems not from overt cultural references,

> **'Japanese designers are known for their peculiar symmetry.'**

but from a shared understanding of cut and lines and a desire to deconstruct. 'Japanese designers are known for their peculiar symmetry, which is probably based on their constant search for variety of form,' explains London-based designer Nicola Woods of the ethical line Beautiful Soul, which reinvents vintage kimonos. 'On dividing a rectangle symmetrically, it would seem that they prefer to use a diagonal line, rather than centrally placing a horizontal or vertical line.'

Opposite Models in creations by Yohji Yamamoto Autumn/Winter 2007, Paris

Kenzo Autumn/Winter 2008, Hong Kong

Models wearing creations by Hanae Mori Autumn/Winter 2004, Tokyo

By way of contrast, Hanae Mori, one of the brightest fashion stars to ever shine out of Japan, launched her career at home. She opened her first atelier in Shinjuku, Tokyo in 1951, and only later opened one in Paris. Hanae Mori is the only Japanese woman to have presented her collections on the runways of Paris and New York, and the first Asian woman to have her haute-couture design house admitted to the Fédération Française de la Couture in France. Mori designed elegant Western-style haute couture for women, which was as popular abroad as it was at home. In the 1990s, she launched a line of *uchikake*, or wedding kimonos, and was asked to design one for Crown Princess Masako's wedding. Mori retired in 2005.

Top Models wearing creations by Hanae Mori Autumn/Winter 2004, Tokyo

Opposite Kenzo Spring/Summer 2011, Paris

Marc Jacobs for Louis Vuitton Spring/Summer 2010, Paris

Marc Jacobs for Louis Vuitton Spring/Summer 2010, Paris

While the country's premier sartorialists continue to reign abroad from their Parisian ateliers, Japan today is a hotbed of fashion activity. *Vogue Nippon* first hit Tokyo newsstands in 1999 and Japan Fashion Week (launched in 2005) has become a platform for the best young talent under the rising sun to strut their stuff. With low production runs and mainly local stockists, designers such as Everlasting Sprout, Né-net (a label under Issey Miyake's broad umbrella) and Limi Feu (daughter of Yohji Yamamoto) cater to the stylish Tokyo girl-at-large. This means a wholehearted espousal of the *kawaii* aesthetic,

in essence the kind of kitchy-cum-cuteness with extraordinary attention to detail for which Japanese street style is famed.

With regards to street style, avid and eager Japanese fashionistas have evolved a street zeitgeist unto themselves. From the posh Harajuku Girls championed by Gwen Stefani to hoards of girls dabbling in various trend movements such as Gothic Lolita (a mixture of the Gothic and Lolita fashions that originated in the 1980s) and Visual Kei (a movement popular with musicians characterized by the use of striking makeup, unusual hairstyles and elaborate costumes, often, but not always, coupled with androgynous aesthetics of the kind also made popular in the 1980s), Japanese street style is amongst the most creative in the world. Marc Jacobs's Spring/Summer 2010 collection for Louis Vuitton tapped into this aesthetic, drawing on the eclecticism of Japanese street style to fuel his vibrant, print-ridden, clashing-pattern, afro-wigged collection. "It was a mix that was non-ethnic but totally ethnic at the same time: a mix of

cultures, street terminology and slang which took on manga-like proportions," Jacobs explained to *Elle* in a 2010 interview.

RECOMMENDED DESIGNERS AND RESOURCES *Japan*

Kenzo Takada
Yohji Yamamoto
Issey Miyake

Rei Kawakubo
Junya Watanabe
Hanae Mori
Everlasting Sprout
Limi Feu
Ne-Net

Alexander McQueen Spring/Summer 2008, Paris

Alexander McQueen Spring/Summer 2008, Paris

Models wearing Chriscelin Paris/ Mood et Moon Spring/Summer 2006, Tokyo

Geta sandal inspired shoes from Kenzo Spring/Summer 2011, Paris

Creation by South
Korean designer
Lie Sang Bong for
Spring/Summer
2008, Paris

Korea

Though today we think of Korea as a land painfully divided, with South Korea a capitalist and democratic country and North Korea a single-party Communist nation under the leadership of Kim Jong Il, but Korea was a firmly united nation until 1948. From the early 10th century all the way up to the 20th century, Korea was ruled by a single government and politically and culturally independent of its neighbours. Accordingly, the basic styles of *hanbok*, or Korean traditional dress, were established at a very early date and have remained essentially unchanged to the present day. Such a solid sartorial grounding allowed for the slow evolution of *hanbok* over time, the development of a national style ethos and aesthetic and the subsequent birth of a vivacious locally driven fashion industry. Since the 1990s, contemporary South Korean fashion designers have no longer attempted to copy or replace the dress forms of previous times, or to slavishly imitate trends flying high on the catwalks of Europe or the US, with the result that fashion design in the country has become something entirely different. Culturally relative, amalgamating national cultural attributes as well as foreign elements, South Korean fashion design is amongst the most avant-garde and compelling in Asia.

Hanbok, like much contemporary South Korean fashion design today, stresses the aesthetic of simplicity, the beauty to be found in the minimal. All *hanbok* is straight-cut and two-dimensional, gaining its voluminous, spherical form only when actually donned by the wearer. Such an aesthetic stems from the Korean desire to reflect Confucian tenets in their sartorial choices: dignity for men and modesty for women. Both men and women wear hip-length *baji jeogori*, or pants and long-sleeved jackets, which are secured at the waist with a pair of ties.

Models walk the runway at the South Korean Traditonal Costume 'HanBok' fashion show 2009, Seoul

Model in traditional South Korean costume

Hanbok is still worn as formal attire at traditional ceremonies, and contemporary designers continue to reinvent their nation's traditional garb. *Hanbok* designer Lee Young Hee, who has earned herself the lofty title of 'Korea's fashion ambassador to the world', made her international debut in Paris in 1993 showing *hanbok*-inspired fashions, and has continued to show there, as well as in New York, ever since.

Alongside their economically powerful neighbours, China and Japan, the formerly united Korea was forced to open up to Europe and to westernize its society at the turn of the 20th century, which also marked the end of the Joseon Dynasty that had lasted some five hundred years. Reformists tried to propel the country into a rapid modernization and westernization, and fashion played a crucial role in this reshaping of national and cultural identity. Western styles soon supplanted traditional ones, as up-to-date international styles were introduced by diplomats and students returning from abroad. Actress Kim Hwal Ran, who returned home after graduating from Boston University, was photographed wearing a flapper dress during the 1920s. Almost overnight, the international flapper style, complete with bobbed hair and short one-piece dresses became synonymous with *sinyeoseong*, the 'new woman'.

The outbreak of the Korean War in 1950, however, brought with it a new element of westernization, and the trend-conscious youth in what became South Korea took their cue from the US military in creating their everyday looks. Women began wearing blouses made from the nylon of recycled parachutes, while donations of clothing sent to South Korea through charities opened the Pandora's box of European-style clothing to the Korean masses.

Designer Nora Noh held the first South Korean fashion show at the Bando Hotel in 1956, just after returning from the United States. She was followed by Choi Kyung-ja. Since there were no professional runway models available, actresses, dancers, singers hit the catwalk. Using domestic silks and European fabrics, Choi Kyung-ja showed off sack dresses, jumper skirts, and suits consisting of a jacket with a tight skirt.

International sensations like Christian Dior's postwar creations made a huge impression on many South Korean designers and consumers. Consequently, South Koreans were inspired by Christian Dior's 'New Look', as well as tight-fitting Chinese *cheongsam* dresses. Oh Hyun-ju, who represented South Korea in the Miss Universe pageant of 1959, caused a sensation with a sumptuous look from Nora Noh based on traditional *hanbok* but infused with Western elements. Noh claimed *hwarang*, the uniform of young men that was popular during the Silla dynasty (57BC–935AD), as the inspiration for this sensational *hanbok*-inspired blue satin *arirang* dress decorated with silver leaf.

By the 1960s, South Korean youth were seen sporting skirts (both mini and maxi), hot pants, jeans and t-shirts. But society in general frowned upon these trends and in 1971 President Park Chung-hee (1917–79) ordered broadcasting companies to censor hippie-styled celebrities and made wearing miniskirts shorter than seven inches above the knee a misdemeanour.

At the same time as Western trends were being checked and curtailed, South Korea looked towards mobilizing a fashion industry of its own. Designers and local tailors were quick to launch their own brands, while the government sponsored the development of national ones. By the end of the 1970s, almost all the specialized tailor's shops and boutiques in Seoul had branded themselves and rolled out eponymous labels.

South Korean fashion designers first showed at Paris Fashion Week in 1985, and the Seoul International Fashion Fair was launched the following year so that South Korea could join the world fashion collection calendar. Since 1989, the Seoul Fashion Artists' Association has presented collections like those of Paris, New York and London twice a year in Seoul.

South Korean fashion design, by this time had established for itself a specific identity both at home and abroad, possessing a special spiritual element.

Models present traditional Korean outfits, Paris, 2003

In Korean aesthetics, simplicity and purity is beauty, and South Korean fashion design often reflects this with its preference for off-white tones, an absence of ornamentation, simple lines and a harmony between black and white.

Designer Lie Sang Bong infuses his fashions with this aesthetic of purity, believing that when the spiritual component of Asian fashion is brought forward, its aesthetic value increases. Using *Hangeul* (the Korean alphabet) and quotes from the *Hunminjongeum* (1446), the first document using this alphabet, Lie Sang Bong literally expresses the timelessness of Korean aesthetic values and culture, which are there for all to see on the fabric pages of his garments. His recent collections, with names like Hangeul Walks on the Moonlight, Moon Light Shadow, and Fiery Fluidity, Water and Fire, convey modern interpretations of Korean ink painting. "Korean

calligraphy dress make people recognize how the Korean Alphabet can be beautifully and naturally embroidered on the clothes, which enables Koreans to make proud of ourselves and our alphabet.

There are also notions of space at work in South Korean fashion design. The spatial characteristic of *hanok*, or the traditional Korean house, is defined as 'layering and interpenetration'. That is to say, the relation between rooms is not one of a closed discontinuation but rather an open continuation and spatial flow, and the layering of garments reflects a similar aesthetic in traditional dress. Even at the stage of pattern cutting, every piece in Korean traditional design, regardless of size or proportion, is a square. When worn, the relation between garments is not between inner and outer layers but rather an open-ended continuity.

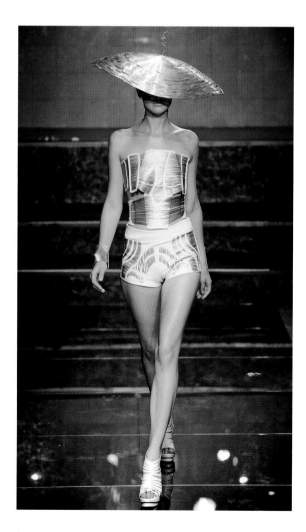

A model showcases designs by Lie Sang Bong at Seoul Fashion Week 2009

Top Designer Lie Sang Bong
Opposite Lie Sang Bong Spring/Summer 2009, Paris

Lee Young Hee Autumn/Winter 2011 at Paris Haute
Couture Fashion Week

Lee Young Hee Autumn/Winter 2011 at Paris Haute
Couture Fashion Week

Fashion designers like Icinoo, Jin Te-ok and Lee Young Hee have captured this traditional aesthetic in their work, perceiving the body as an abstract form, describing it two dimensionally and playing with concepts of formlessness. For example, Icinoo's garments are so deconstructed that they frequently have minimal form. Sometimes the inside becomes the outside or vice versa. It's hard to tell where the traditional components of garments begin and end, as all becomes one unified whole: sleeves transform into bodices, a clear line suddenly becomes a broken one. Korean designers are ever-conscious of this concept of space and flow, and fashion's relationship to interiors, so much so that Jin Te-ok once used black models against a black background on the runway to create the optical illusion of limitless space.

Thus South Korean fashion design transforms the spiritual values of traditional culture into visible form for contemporary global audiences, underscoring the fact that, despite the country's continued state of political unrest and division, in fashion terms the design aesthetic and vision draws from an outlook that was once shared by North and South alike.

RECOMMENDED DESIGNERS AND RESOURCES *Korea*

Lie Sang-Bong
Lee Young Hee

Nora Noh
Choi Kyung-Ja
Icinoo
Jin Te-ok

Southeast Asia: Indonesia, Philippines, Vietnam, Thailand

Southeast Asia, a large, culturally rich region comprised of many diverse nations and ethnic groups, has a long-held fascination for the Western fashion designer. It is a region whose textiles, fabrics, embroidery and embellishment techniques inspire the ateliers of Paris to find striking effects of colour and print, and different kinds of wrapping and layering. Locally, fashion has been shaped by various colonial influences, a clash of cultures which manifested in new kinds of dress, fermenting the seeds of a creative fashion industry. Indonesia, the Philippines and Vietnam in particular, since throwing off their colonial powers – respectively, the Dutch, the Spanish and then the Americans, and the French – have been using fashion to assert their national identities. Since the area has for so long been at the crossroads of trade and the confluence of cultures, fashion today, both on local runways and on the streets, is very much a stylized hybrid of traditional regional and modern Western styles. An interesting blend of ethnic dress will always continue to be worn on formal occasions such as cultural festival days and national holidays. But a healthy crop of talented designers, both at home and showing on major runways abroad, has helped to create a burgeoning fashion industry in the region, one with its own uniquely chic ethnic style.

Model parades an outfit during a fashion show at Indonesia National Textile Exhibition 2008

Model displays a creation by Vietnamese designer Minh Hanh Spring/Summer 2009, Rome

Etro Spring/Summer 2011, Milan

Matthew Williamson Spring/Summer 2008, London

Indonesia

Land of the batik, a painstaking fabric decoration technique which has graced many a spring/summer catwalk, Indonesia is much more than just a holiday destination for the fashion industry. With more than 17,000 islands and over 300 ethnic groups – each with their own dress traditions – Indonesia's fashion footprint is one of unique cultural diversity that has served to inspire a myriad of European designers who have visited its white sand beaches and crystal clear waters.

> '*Indonesian designers, particularly the older generation are very influenced by our rich culture, which makes their clothes sometimes are not practical enough for day-to-day wear.*'

Dutch colonial influence on Indonesian dress is specific in character on account of the influential *Indische* culture, comprising people of mixed Dutch and Indonesian parentage. Being neither wholly Asian nor wholly white, the *Indische* under Dutch rule were granted European status and with it the option to don Western garb. Since the Dutch were importing white cottons from India, England and the Netherlands to be used in the batik industry, a new Eurasian fusion style, *batik belanda* (*belanda* meaning 'the Netherlands'), quickly gained enormous popularity within the *Indische* culture.

Batik is essentially inextricable from most resort lines and has even spawned a cult brand all unto itself, Paris-based Antik Batik. Countless designers, including Nicole Miller (inspired by her assistant's

A batik craftswoman applies melted wax to a fine cotton textile to produce characteristic figurative designs

Outfit by
Belgian designer
Dries Van Noten
Spring/Summer
2010, Paris

Creation by
Riccardo Tisci
for Givenchy
Haute Couture
Autumn/Winter
2006, Paris

Creation by Indonesian designer Denny Wirawan at Jakarta Fashion Week 2009

Etro Spring/Summer 2011, Milan

travels to Bali for Resort 2006), Matthew Williamson (reinterpreting the batik as a pinstripe in schoolboy short suits for Spring/Summer 2008), Dries Van Noten (Spring/Summer 2010), Michael Kors and Veronica Etro for her family's eponymous line, Etro (Resort 2010 and Spring/Summer 2009 respectively), have voyaged to Bali or elsewhere in Indonesia to return with their heads awash with intricate batiks. Givenchy's Ricardo Tisci has a particular penchant for Indonesian batik-style prints, and featured them in both Givenchy's Autumn/Winter 2006 Couture and Spring/Summer 2007 Ready-to-Wear collections. In fact, the contribution of batiks to the European creative scene at large over the centuries has been so great that in 2009 UNESCO recognized its production and that of *ikat* (another textile created from a resist-dye method) as Masterpieces of the Oral and Intangible Heritage of Humanity.

> *'The new crop of designers are especially relentless in introducing ready-to-wear looks that are inspired by traditional clothes like the kebaya top worn with jeans.'*

Fashion designers such as Iwan Tirta have vigorously introduced batik into the global fashion scene and worked to promote the Indonesian art of batik dress in its traditional and modern forms at home. Jakarta held its first fashion week in August 2008. Each season is themed and the show organizers always encourage the young designers to reach into their culture for inspiration. Models sashayed down the runways sporting European-style cuts in an array of traditional fabrics created by the country's leading designers, such as Sebastian Gunawan, Biyan Wanaatmadja, Musa Widyatmojo, Taruna K. Kusmayadi, Putu Aliki, Jeanny Ang, Lenny Agustin, Carmanita, Ghea Sukasah, Edward (Edo) Hutabarat and Denny Wirawan Bali had launched its own fashion week seven years earlier, but the management decided to axe the event in 2009 due to the global economic crisis.

"Indonesian designers, particularly the older generation are very influenced by our rich culture, which makes their clothes sometimes are not practical enough for day-to-day wear," explains

Etro Spring/
Summer 2011,
Milan

Doutzen Kroes
wearing Nicole
Miller Spring/
Summer 2007,
New York

Nicole Miller
Spring/Summer
2007, New York

Hanifa Ambadar, Editor-in-Chief of Fashionese Daily, Indonesia's premier fashion blog, launched in 2005. "They often makes clothes with beads, luxurious fabrics and cuts that make anyone who wear them stand out from the crowd. But [a new generation of] designers are making [ranges with] cheaper price range and styles that are more wearable. The new crop of designers are especially relentless in introducing ready-to-wear looks that are inspired by traditional clothes like the *kebaya* top worn with jeans … Or making batik look hip and young like the Jeffry Tan and Geulis labels for instance."

Poverty remains widespread in Indonesia today and can be readily seen in the enormous gulf in styles of dress between urban and rural areas. Traditional loincloths are still worn by elderly men deep in the interior of Kalimantan (the Indonesian part of the island of Borneo), while the young and rich in Jakarta sport Armani trousers and Gucci shoes. Women, for the most part, dress modestly as Indonesia has a very large Muslim population.

However, despite the limitations with which both Indonesian designers and consumers have to cope, Hanifa Ambadar is optimistic about her country's future place on the global fashion stage. "Right now," she explains, "new designers have started to export their clothes to independent boutiques in neighbouring countries like Singapore and Malaysia –for example Stella Rissa, Nikicio, Priyo. Some, like Kleting, work together with Harvey Nichols department store to create special lines. Aranxta Adi, has also just been chosen to be the designer for [American premium denim label] Citizen of Humanity, and Indonesian designer Ardistia is also making it big in New York."

Opposite Models display creations by Indonesian designer Denny Wirawan at Jakarta Fashion Week 2009

Top Model wearing dress by Sebastian Gunawan at Jakarta Fashion Week 2009

RECOMMENDED DESIGNERS AND RESOURCES *Indonesia*	
Antik Batik	Jeanny Ang
Iwan Tirta	Lenny Agustin
Sebastian Gunawan	Carmanita
Biyan Wanaatmadja	Ghea Sukasah
Musa Widyatmojo	Edward (Edo) Hutabarat
Taruna K. Kusmayadi	Denny Wirawan
Putu Aliki	Jeffry Tan & Geulis
	Stella Rissa
	Nikicio
	Priyo

Philippines

It's the home to famous fashion exports as various as footwear legend Imelda Marcos (and her 3000 pairs of shoes), international super-blogger BryanBoy, and Hollywood A-listers' go-to red-carpet designer Monique L'Huillier. But back home, a new generation of Filipino designers are looking more introspectively into their own culture toward the evolution of their own national fashion identity.

The *barong tagalog* and *baro't saya* are the country's national costume, though these garments have been much influenced over the years by the colonial powers in the Philippines – the Spanish and then the Americans. The *barong tagalog*, worn traditionally by men, is a sort of embroidered lightweight shirt made from a variety of soft materials such as *piña* (pineapple fibre) and banana fibre fabric, and is worn untucked. During the Spanish period, the *barong tagalog* saw changes to its collar, cuffs and fit,

responding to Western trends. Since the late 20th century, the *barong tagalog* has been worn by men only on official and special personal occasions such as weddings. However, casual everyday versions abound in the form of polo *barong*s, linen *barong*s and even shirt-jack *barong*s.

The *baro't saya*, the traditional costume for women, is a two-piece outfit consisting of a layered blouse (*baro*) and a long skirt (*saya*). Under Spanish colonial rule, the basic look evolved into a many-layered ensemble with as many as five separate garments worn at once, despite the balmy climate. The Maria Clara style was a 19th-century incarnation of the *baro't saya* with a Spanish twist, which featured a transparent blouse with exaggerated bell sleeves matched with a Victorian-style flared skirt and topped off with a *pañuelo* or *alampay*–a large kerchief or shawl wrapped around the shoulders.

The show collection of Imelda Marcos

Imelda Marcos, First Lady of the Philippines, 1972

Trophy Oconpo and Helena Luchauso wear traditional dress during a UN party, 1948

Designer Monique L'Hullier

Fashion design pioneer Ramon Valera revived the style as a bridal gown in the 1950s. Twenty years before, the avant-garde designer had been credited with removing the *pañuelo* and train from the *terno* and turning it into a one-piece evening gown, to the distaste of the older generation. The *terno*, which is also an Spanish American word for a suit, alludes to the combination of blouse and skirt, but is actually made from multiple cuts of the same fabric seamlessly joined at the waist to form a one-piece dress. The sleeves distinguish the *terno*, with sculpted shoulders that stand upright like clipped butterfly wings, perhaps a precursor to the Western trend for shoulder pads. The concept is essentially the same; the exaggeration of the shoulder and the nipped-in waist of the *terno* flatter the wearer, making her more shapely, just as shoulder pads were teamed with high-waisted skirts on European catwalks in the 1980s.

As first lady from the 1960s to the 1980s, Imelda Marcos appropriated the *terno* as her signature look, wearing it to almost all formal gatherings. Wives of important government officials followed suit. After 21 years under the government of Imelda's husband, Ferdinand Marcos, the popularity of the *terno* waned after the People Power revolution ousted the couple in 1986; together with her enormous collection of shoes, it had come to symbolize a stigmatized political affiliation and the unbridled decadence that had gone with it.

Today, young Filipino designers are looking hopefully towards the creation of a successful domestic fashion industry. Philippine Fashion Week launched with four catwalk shows in a shopping mall in 1997, but is now the biggest fashion event in the country, showcasing the work of 100 designers. Aesthetically, the designers still look to their mixed

Model shows a design by Filipino designer
Alfonso Guino-O, 2006

BryanBoy at Dolce and Gabbana Spring/Summer 2011, Milan

heritage, adding Filipino touches or an Asian essence to Western-style dress – for example, giving a wide tribal neckline to a t-shirt, wrapping a *tapis,* a rectangular piece of cloth used to wrap around the body, as an outer skirt around a slip dress, or printing a body stocking with colorful tribal weaving patterns. There has also been a revival in the production and quality of fabrics largely unique to the Philippines, such as those made from *piña, ramie* and *abaca* fibres. Designers such as Inno Soto, Rajo Laurel and Dita Sandico Ong have used bamboo silk textiles in their contemporary designs. For these reasons, Filipino fashion is seen in the region as cutting-edge Southeast Asian style.

RECOMMENDED DESIGNERS AND RESOURCES
Philippines

Ramon Valera
Inno Soto
Rajo Laurel
Dita Sandico Ong

Vietnam

The *ao dai*, a tight-fitting full-length, long-sleeved tunic, is the national dress of Vietnam, and also a silhouette found in Western fashion. In 1930 the Vietnamese fashion designer Cat Tuong, known to the French as Monsieur Le Mur, updated the garment for a more modern, Western era. He lengthened the *ao dai* so that the top garment reached the floor and hugged the curves closer to the body. Over time, the shape became more and more form-fitting.

The collarless *ao dai* style was popularized by the infamous Madame Ngo Dinh Nhu (former First Lady of South Vietnam). The *ao dai* is featured in an array of Vietnam-themed or -related movies.

A creation by Bui Hong Phuong for the Vietnam Collection Grand Prix 2007 contest 2007

A Vu Thanh Hoa design for the Vietnam Collection Grand Prix 2008

Vietnamese
woman in
traditional *ao dai*
dress with
conical hat

Model displays
a creation by
Vietnamese
designer Minh
Hanh Spring/
Summer 2009,
Rome

Top left Models wearing designs by Ha Duy at the Vietnam Collection Grand Prix 2008

Top right Creation by Nguyen Quang Huy for Vietnam's national fashion design contest Vietnam Collection – Grand Prix 2004

Bottom Front row seats at the Da-Nang Spring/Summer 2005 show in California

The 1992 films *Indochine* and *The Lover* inspired several international fashion houses to design *ao dai* collections, including Prada's Spring/Summer 2008 collection. Designer Sy Hoang is regarded by many as the modern master of the *ao dai* and is a celebrity in Vietnam. Others, like Minh Hanh and Vo Viet Chung, continue to inspire a new generation of designers through the annual Vietnam Collection Grand Prix fashion competition.

RECOMMENDED DESIGNERS AND RESOURCES
Vietnam

Cat Tuong
Sy Hoang
Minh Hanh
Vo Viet Chung

Thailand

For a long time the words 'Thailand' and 'fashion' appearing in the same sentence would conjure up for many Westerners ideas of crowded street stalls bustling with printed silks, textiles and – most importantly for some – fake designer goods. But Thai influence on fashion from couture to streetwear, be it as subtle as a bit of decorative embroidery or as direct as an ornate headpiece, is certainly there, though at first it may not be easily distinguished from more general Southeast Asian themes.

Because Thailand shares borders with three countries – Burma to the west and north, Cambodia to the southeast and Malaysia to the south – the development of Thai dress was shaped by the constant exchange of cultures coming together at the country's borders. The Chinese influenced dress through trade and invasion, while Indian forms of dress, such as the sarong, were adopted by Thais in the west and south of the country. As immigrants poured into Thailand over the centuries, bringing with them their own cultures and religions, the Thais' own dress and ornamentation were changed by these influences.

Minority ethnic people who settled along the Thai border, pouring into the country over a thousand years ago from southern China through Laos, Burma and Vietnam, are known collectively as the hill tribes. Each tribe has its own distinct culture, religion, language and arts and a lot of what we in the West think of as Thai-influenced fashion stems in fact from these highland people. These hill tribes have created rich textiles representing their unique aesthetic in

Long neck Padaung hill tribe woman

Hill tribes women in traditional costume

fashion and clothing, which have influenced leading fashion's printmakers such as Dries Van Noten and Diane von Fürstenberg. They decorate garments with small silver plates, like large sequins, a staple form of embellishment in what has become known as the tribal style – a bit of adornment at the neck of a printed maxi from Tory Burch, for example. Women of the Long-Necked Karen tribe are known for wearing layers of coiled bangles encircling their necks, the number of which is gradually added to as a child grows to extend the length of her neck. This trend has often been imitated by jewellers – Pebble London, for example – as an aspect of Tribal Chic.

Typical traditional Thai dress consists of lengths of fabric folded, wrapped and draped to fit comfortably to the body, influenced by the warm tropical climate. A wrapped cloth could also be used to form a shawl to protect and conceal the upper body. Since the basic garments were so simple, Thais accessorized and embellished their clothes with embroidery, buttons,

gold-thread brocade or inlaid precious stones. Body piercing and tattooing was also a major part of self-decoration, varying by region and remaining popular to this day. For men, body decorations that displayed masculinity were believed to provide protection on the battlefield. Angelina Jolie had a 12-inch long, 8-inch wide Bengal tiger tattooed on her lower back in Bangkok to commemorate her Cambodian citizenship. The tiger tattoo, which represents vigour and physical force, was done in the traditional Thai tattoo style with a manual needle.

For men, *pha chong kraben*, or long-style wrapping trousers were adopted by Thai society in the Sukhothai period (1238–1438) from Cambodian dress. Cut from a single rectangular piece of material, the wearer would wrap the fabric around his body, tying it at the waist and rolling or folding the excess fabric between the legs from front to back, where he would then twist it and tuck it in at the waist. These are the basis for the menswear skirts-for-men trend as seen on the runway at the Y-3 show for Adidas in September 2008. The following season Yohji Yamamoto showed a long, billowing version on the menswear runways in his main line, while Yves Saint Laurent, Jean Paul Gaultier and Alexander McQueen showed more tailored styles of the same garment. Even H&M followed suit with a high-street version.

In traditional Thai society women were not allowed to reveal their upper bodies, and so concealed them with shawl-like wrappers. The *sabai*, which was a fabric made of pleated silk or gold brocade, is one kind of popular decorative wrapper which is often copied in the West. *Sabai* are draped over the shoulder and fall loosely over the back, fluttering as the wearer walks or moves. Valentino, for one, created a pair of sumptuous embellished red silk separates for his Spring/Summer 2005 couture show in Paris, and topped off the look with a wispy red *sabai* around the model's neck.

In the Rattanakosin period (1782–1932), high-ranking people and members of the nobility adopted Western tailored garments. Trade and new religions spurred change. Although Thailand was never colonized by a European power, Western styles of clothing were readily adopted and became fashionable. Tailored garments gradually replaced wrapping cloths as the everyday form of dress. By the early 21st century, Western dress had prevailed, with fully decorated wrapping clothes becoming ever rarer such that they are now only brought out for performances of traditional dance or for special occasions such as weddings.

Today, Thailand is looking towards propelling itself onto the global fashion stage. Bangkok held

Thai students dressed in traditional costumes in front of the Royal Pavilion, 2006

Thakoon Spring/Summer 2010, New York

Thakoon Spring/Summer 2010, New York

Koi Suwannagate Spring/Summer 2009, New York

Princess Sirivannavari Nariratana walks the catwalk at the end of her collection during Elle Fashion Week 2008, Bangkok

its first fashion week in 2005 and Thai expats Koi Suwannagate and Thakoon Panichgul, both based in New York, are major players on the scene. Koi Suwannagate, who has a bachelor's degree in art, not fashion design, perfectly intertwines gestures towards her heritage with complex inspirations from 'nature's texture and form' and an eye for 'architecure and imperfection'. Suwannagate's telltale Thai influences lie in the details of her intricate garments and their handcrafted sensibilities. 'I grew up in a house where people like to make up things by hands … surrounded with the soft nature and elegance of the art of handcraft,' she explains '[Textiles as a] labour of love and custom handmade cloth was what I grew up with … [so] the influence of [traditional] handcraft lies deep in my soul.'

> *'It's not about the traditional Thai dress, it's more about the Thai culture and how we see things over here – easy and eclectic.'*

Even the royal family has a penchant for style – Princess Sirivannavari Nariratana, the youngest child and only daughter of Crown Prince Maha Vajiralongkorn, is herself a fashion designer. In 2007, at the age of 20, she was invited by French couturier Pierre Balmain to present her collection Presence of the Past, a modern interpretation of traditional Thai design, at Paris Fashion Week.

Designer Nagara Sambandaraksa has entered into partnership with legendary silk producer Jim Thompson to produce an innovative ready-to-wear line, resplendent with elongated Machu-era gowns and vibrant, sensual eastern jewel tones. Nagara Sambandaraksa, official designer to Thailand's Queen Sirikit and the darling of Bangkok's 'hi-so' (high society), studied textile design in Britain and so infuses his work with the tension of East meets West. Many of his prints embody the DNA of ancient

Y-3 fashion show 2008, New York

Designer Koi Suwannagate

Thai murals, and he has revitalized traditional *ikat*, an ancient weaving technique that laces pre-dyed threads into a blurred 'underwater' design.

Thailand is also brimming with young talent. One successful up-and-comer is designer Sretsis (the word 'sisters' spelled backward), the girly and quirky label of Pimdao 'Pim' Sukhahuta, who was born in Bangkok in 1979 and then studied in New York at Parsons School of Design. After only three years in the business, her label had become a national favorite with young, stylish girls, and it currently has stockists in both Hong Kong and the UK, has been featured on the pages of *Teen Vogue* and *Nylon*, and is a favorite with pop star Katy Perry. "To me," explains Sukhahuta when asked about whether her work incorporates her ethnicity, "it's not about the traditional Thai dress, it's more about the Thai culture and how we see things over here – easy and eclectic. There is always a sense of craftsmanship and sentimental humour in my work and I assume that comes from being Thai."

Tipayaphong Poosanaphong is another to watch – he got his start as a lowly button sorter in a Paris fashion house then graduated to working alongside Emanuel Ungaro before returning to Thailand to launch his own line. Designer Munchumart Numbenjapol of the alternative fashion brand Munchu's emerged on the scene in 2004, producing pieces so unique that each collection is made-to-order only, though still surprisingly affordable.

When asked about the future of Thai fashion, Koi Suwannagate replied matter-of-factly, "Thai fashion will always adopt what is in fashion and [re]make it in our own way."

RECOMMENDED DESIGNERS AND RESOURCES
Thailand

Koi Suwannagate
Thakoon Panichgul
Princess Sirivannavari
Nariratana

Nagara Sambandaraska
Sretsis
Tipayaphong
Poosanaphong
Munchu

Model in
an outfit by
designer Sretsis
at Rosemount
Australian
Fashion Week
Spring/Summer
2008, Sydney

Model in an outfit
by designer Sretsis
at Rosemount
Australian Fashion
Week Spring/
Summer 2008,
Sydney

Thakoon
Autumn/Winter
2010,
New York

Indian woman with henna decorated hands

India

India's fashion culture, as well as its place on the global fashion stage, is very much representative of the fact that the country, home to over a billion people, where massive gulfs in social and economic conditions separate the urban rich from the rural poor, is very much a nation comprised of two worlds. A Bollywood actress swathed head to toe in Gucci, a model prancing about in a Rajesh Pratap Singh dress, a politician in *khadi kurta* (a loose collarless shirt made of homespun cloth) or a woman in traditional garments – there is a place for each in India's fashion scene. And its influences on the West – from the straightforward donation of the sari to the dazzling gems of the maharajas to the Kashmir shawl and the invention of the paisley print, right down to henna tattoos, turbans and *chappals* (the Indian manifestation of the flip-flop) – greatly outnumber those of many of its Asian neighbours.

India's history, from the birth of Buddha to the death of Gandhi, is a rich and diverse one shaped by a long history of cultural exchange across its borders. Accordingly, its history of dress mirrors this influx of neighbouring cultures (China and Nepal to the north, Bangladesh and Burma to the east). Kushan rule (60–375AD) established Central Asian influence, bringing with it a larger range of stitched garments (as opposed to the sari, which actually means 'unstitched length of cloth'). Alexander the Great's invasion (327BC) introduced the concept of draped dress and also highly evolved jewellery – gold filigree and elaborate settings, for example. The establishment of the Turkish sultanate (1206–1527) brought Muslim codes of dress, including the *burqa*, into India. Finally, the colonization of undivided India by the British and their educational system led to the eventual Westernization of everyday dress in urban centres.

Sari factory in Rajasthan, India

Gold Indian bangles on purple sari cloth

Since the times of Alexander the Great, the West has viewed India as a land replete with wealth, whose soil teems with rubies, diamonds and emeralds. Hence, the history of India's culture of gems and jewels continues to shape contemporary jewellery design today. Historically, in India jewellery showed the wearer's social status, material wealth, caste, religion and area of origin. Jewels functioned as symbols of the power of the divine, while precious stones were also used for their medicinal and therapeutic properties – *Ayurveda*, for example, was a branch of ancient Indian life science that makes extensive use of gem and gold therapy.

From the 1850s the West became enraptured with what they saw as Oriental exoticism, and a newfound fascination with Indian gems and jewellery resulted in a cross-fertilization of jewellery designs, forms and techniques. Indian maharajas succumbed to the lure of Cartier, the French jewellers, and handed over their family heirlooms to be reset in the new Western style. Cartier created an entirely new genre of jewels for the maharaja (recreated by Alexander McQueen in the form of the exquisite so-called Maharajah

necklaces, chandelier earrings and diadems that accompanied the Autumn/Winter 2008 collection). They amalgamated the bold colours of Indian enamel with the art-deco styles created by their designers, as well as drawing on centuries-old classical Indian design motifs and forms, adapting and incorporating them into the Western design idiom to produce a new style of jewellery. Other French jewellers, such as Boucheron, Van Cleef & Arpels, and Chopard, as well as English jewellers such as Garrard, also recast the gems of Indian royalty and introduced Indian-inspired jewellery to their Western clientele.

The Kashmir shawl is another of India's great contributions to global fashion, the precursor for printed scarves as essential fashion accessories. Woven in twill tapestry from the finest trans-Himalayan goat *pashm* (cashmere), the shawl made its first appearance in Europe near the end of 18th century, when officials of the East India Company brought back a few pieces for their wives. European imitations were being woven on the recently invented Jacquard loom (whose technological sophistication encouraged patterns that covered the entire textile)

'*Women wear their saris with such creative ease; the soft silhouette; the flowing fabric; the layering of textures and flashes of embellishment.*'

and soon a craze was born. The sleepy Scottish town of Paisley wound up becoming the shawl production capital of Europe, and the term 'paisley' had become synonymous not only with shawls themselves but also with the derivations of the *buta* or floral motif that had evolved over a period of several years in the ateliers of the Kashmiri shawl designers.

Though it was and still is common practice to walk barefoot in rural areas, India has contributed two important shapes to the development of international fashion footwear: the *chappal* and the *mojari*. *Chappals* are worn by men, women and children of all religions and social strata, and date back as far as the first century AD. Sometimes ornamented with jewels or other embellishments, the sandals feature a strap which forms a toe ring to hold the foot in place. Chappals remain popular today as designer and high-street versions abound in the West, season after season. The *mojari*, or Indian slipper, is a shoe made of coloured leather, featuring low sides, pointed toes and low heels. *Mojaris* exist in a wide range of styles that evolved over the centuries across the South Asian subcontinent. Aristocrats traditionally wore velvet ones with long, flattened, upturned toes. These were embroidered with smooth gold or silver wire, sequins, beads, pearls, iridescent beetles' wings and precious stones. Mojaris usually have no left–right distinction and may be flat-soled or fashioned with a small heel. The back is often folded down or removed altogether. Alexander McQueen shod models in elaborate versions of the shoe for his Autumn/Winter 2008 collection, which was inspired by the British Raj period.

Alexander McQueen Autumn/Winter 2008, Paris

Indian woman in a sari, surrounded by sari fabric and decoarated with henna tattoos, jewellery and bindi

Indian model
in traditional
inspired sari by
Manish Malhotra
at Kolkata
Fashion Week
2009

Last, but most certainly not least, the sari, the famous traditional dress of Indian women, has had a colossal influence on Western runways. Ann Demeulemeester (Autumn/Winter 2006), Chaiken (Autumn/Winter 2007), Costume National (Spring/Summer 2008), Hermès (Spring/Summer 2008), Alexander McQueen (Autumn/Winter 2008) and Etro (Spring/Summer 2009) are among the many who have looked to the garment for inspiration. On the red carpet, Elizabeth Hurley, caused a stir when she attended a charity fundraiser in 2010 in a translucent blue sari without a *choli* or *ravika*, the cropped top normally worn underneath to cover up.

The sari recently also enjoyed an special resurgence on the runways for Spring/Summer 2010. Carolina Herrera, Amanda Wakeley, Kenzo and Chanel couture utilized the eye popping bright colours typical of Indian fabrics, as well as one-shoulder sari silhouettes. "'I was passionately inspired by traditionally dressed Indian men and women,'" Amanda Wakeley told the *Financial Times* in an interview in 2010. "'The way the women wear their saris with such creative ease; the soft silhouette; the flowing fabric; the layering of textures and flashes of embellishment.'"

But the credit for the popularity enjoyed by the sari on the catwalks of Europe and America belongs entirely to eccentric British designer Zandra Rhodes, who experimented with the shape in the late 1980s and describes her particular style as centring on how 'printed textiles can be used differently'. She produced long, sari-like dresses with bizarre motifs

Ann Demeulemeester Autumn/Winter 2006, Paris

Chaiken Autumn/Winter 2007, New York

Kenzo Spring/Summer 2010, Paris

Indian print dress design for Etro Spring/Summer 2009, Milan

created with sequins and embroidery, as well as uneven hemlines, interesting closures, and blouses with massive shoulder pads of the variety that were so in vogue at the time.

'I think the way I incorporate handmade elements in my work is uniquely Indian.'

'I was first asked to work with the HHEC (Handicraft & Handlooms Export Corporation) in India for the first Festival of India in 1982. To prepare for this I was escorted around India by Rajeev Sethi and fell in love with India,' Rhodes recalled. 'I did two major spectacular catwalk shows in London: The Indian Collection (Autumn/Winter 1982) and India Revisited (Autumn/Winter 1985). I did an Indian-inspired show at The Grosvenor House Hotel for an Indian charity. It was attended by a very glamorous Indian audience. None of them wore Western dress and most were in saris! When I mingled amongst the audience I realized that what I was showing would not be bought or worn by everyone in this audience

… And so I embarked upon my sari adventure! To do a range of exotic saris to appeal to the world and the Indian audience. Additionally, as I was a textile designer I began to see the sari as a magnificent garment that I would reinterpret and look at with both textile and fashion Western eyes.'

In 1987, when Zhandra Rhodes launched the designer saris in Bombay (now Mumbai) and Delhi, not only were they considered avant-garde in Europe and the US, but such an unorthodox reinterpretation of the traditional national garment shocked the Indian public. Her 'designer saris', aside from positioning Indian dress as major cultural influence from which Western ready-to-wear should draw, also inspired an entire generation of young Indian fashion designers who dared to explore the sari still further.

"My friend and Indian mentor Rajeev had to help win over many people of the old school from being so shocked," Rhodes recalls. "I made a *salwah*

Jean Paul Gaultier
for Hermes
Spring/Summer
2008, Paris

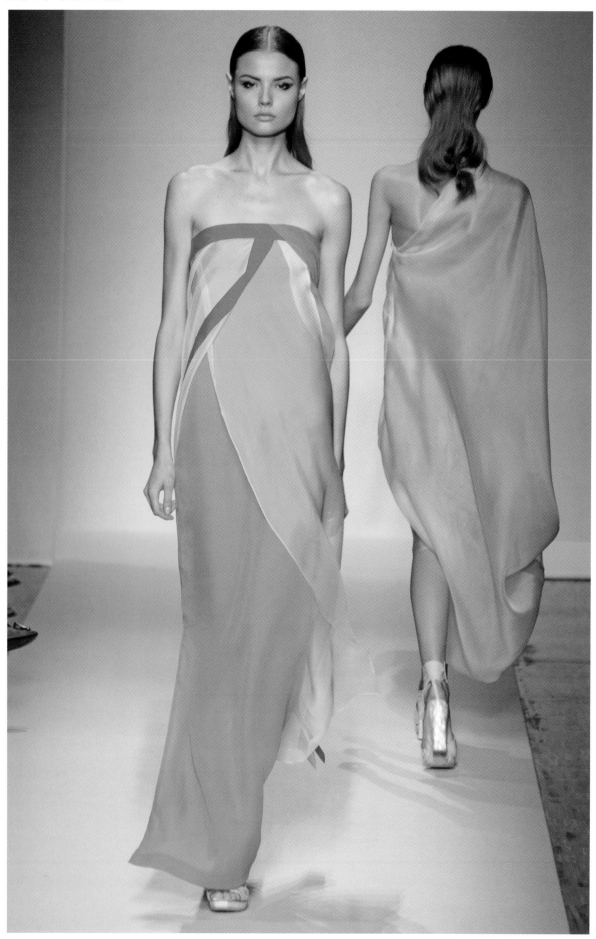

Costume National
Spring/Summer
2008, Paris

Model wears
Indian textile
patterned dress
for Hermes
Spring/Summer
2008, Paris

Model wears
Indian inspired
costume with
traditional pattern
for Etro
Spring/Summer
2009, Milan

chemise with shoulder pads and puffed sleeves! I did some of them one-sided (the native *salwah* chemises were just plain fitted sleeves)! I studied all the different ways a sari could be tied so I could tie them absolutely correctly–but in the catwalk show, I showed one group with panniers, walking sticks and with ostrich-feather headdresses. Another sari had beaded holes through which the women could look and have different choices of which hole to put both arms and head through."

Thus, a new era of Indian style was ushered in, building on the platform for fashion provided by Bollywood, the Hindi film industry based in Mumbai. Essentially, the evolution of contemporary fashion design as well as popular street styles in India can be tracked alongside the development of Bollywood. Its impact on fashion has been mammoth: from the 1950s on, the elite

and the masses alike have sought to emulate the dress of Bollywood's heroines and heroes.

Another important impact on the development of the Indian fashion industry has been the richness of traditional crafts and textiles (processes of dyeing, printing, embroidery and embellishment) and their interaction with Western sensibilities. Indian designers today use handcrafting in some form or another while producing fashion apparel and textiles, lending a cultural authenticity to their designs. They interpret traditional styling, tie-dye techniques, hand embroidery like *chikankari* and *zardozi*, and fine sewing techniques to create contemporary fashion.

Young designer Varun Sardana, for example, does not generally draw on traditional Indian dress in his designs but emphasizes that his culture comes through in the handcrafted details. "'I think the

British model Lily Cole in sari inspired outfit by Jean Paul Gaultier for Hermes Spring/Summer 2008, Paris

Carolina Herrara Spring/Summer 2010, New York

Ashish Gupta walks the runway after his Spring/Summer 2011 fashion show, London

way I incorporate handmade elements in my work is uniquely Indian,'" he explains. "'We have a wealth of traditional skills which can be adapted very well for contemporary fashion, which gives us an edge over our contemporaries in the West.'" The Western notion of fashion as 'wearable art' has also encouraged textile designers in India to focus on a clever fusion of tradition and modernity. Indian designer Satya Paul, for example, designed saris incorporating motifs and patterns taken from nature, abstract paintings, the many moods of a day, haiku verses, Sufi poetry, and messages of peace from Guru Bhagwan Rajneesh.

'Manish Arora is perfection and provocation.'

India's blossoming local fashion industry also owes a lot to the fact that early on the government recognized its economic potential (the textile industry alone employs 35 million people today) and so set up a number of institutes to train personnel. The National Institute of Fashion Technology (NIFT), established in New Delhi in 1986 has spawned some of India's finest designers – J.J. Valaya, Rajesh Pratap Singh, Manish Arora and Ashish Soni, to name a few. In recent years, NIFT's graduates have included prolific and talented designers like Sabyasachi Mukherjee, Shyam Narayan Prasad, Gaurav Gupta and the afore-mentioned Varun Sardana.

Today, biannual fashion weeks are held in India to accommodate the vast number of young designers itching to break out onto both the Indian and international scenes. "India definitely has been developing its own individual fashion scene, selling to a hungry developing home market," remarks Zhandra Rhodes.

"'There has been a sudden explosion of designers in the past five years and with the advent of the international fashion brands into the country, the domestic retail space has become increasingly competitive,'" expounds Vardun Sardana whilst pondering the future of his country's fashion industry. "'Eventually, I think only those labels that have a definite signature will survive. Also, once any Indian label makes it big internationally, we will see a sea change in the way the industry functions and hopefully that will lead to the industry being more organized.'"

The two well-known fashion weeks–the Wills Lifestyle India Fashion Week (WIFW) and the Lakme India Fashion Week (LIFW) – are held in Delhi and

Model wears
Indian themed
pop art print
dress for Manish
Arora Spring/
Summer 2008,
Paris

Manish Arora Spring/Summer 2008, Paris

Manish Arora Autumn/Winter 2007, London

Mumbai. Indian designers and designers of the Indian diaspora, such as Toronto-born, London-based Ashish Gupta, continue to represent their country on the international calendar of shows. In 2007, designers Manish Arora and Anamika Khanna were the first to present their collections at Paris Fashion Week under their own labels. While Arora showcased the 1970s style in a riot of colours, Khanna's collections used rich Indian colours and displayed a contemporary version of India.

There's no denying the exceptional talent that has come out of India and given the country its modern sartorial identity, a major achievement in the short time since Rhodes's designer saris first appeared. In 2007, Didier Grumbach, President of the Fédération Française de la Couture du Prêt-à-Porter des Couturiers et des Créateurs de Mode,

invited one of these bright young Indian designers, Manish Arora, to show his Spring/Summer 2008 collection at Paris Fashion Week. He had this to say about the designer: "Manish Arora is perfection and provocation. His collection[s] [are] not folkloric but at the same time, could only have been designed by an Indian fashion designer.'"

RECOMMENDED DESIGNERS AND RESOURCES *India*	Manish Arora
	Ashish Soni
	Sabyasachi Mukherjee
	Shyam Narayan Prasad
	Gaurav Gupta
Varun Sardana	Ashisha Gupta
J.J. Valaya	Anamika Khanna
Rajesh Pratrap Singh	

Top left Creation by Indian designer Rajesh Pratap Singh for Spring/Summer 2010 during Wills India Fashion Week

Top right Indian models in creations by Anamika Khanna during India Couture Week 2008, Mumbai

Bottom Model in outfit by Indian designer Anamika Khanna at the Fashion Extravaganza, part of the International Indian Film Academy Awards 2009

the americas

Introduction

The Americas, the New World, the land of promise and adventure opened up to Europe at the end of the 15th century has given birth to a variety of garb and garment as vast as the landmass that stretches from the Bering Strait in the north to that of Magellan in the south. This includes everything from the China poblanas of Mexico to the rich woven textiles and indigenous ponchos of the Andes, from the world-renowned Panama hat to the elaborate appliqué *molas* of the Kuna people and the intricate bead and leatherwork of the Native Americans inhabiting the plains of what is now the United States, The Americas have formed the backdrop to the archetypal clash of cultures, where encounters between long-established tribes and European invaders gave rise, not only to a new mestizo race, but also to a sense of attire that was deeply rooted in the new cultural combinations.

The peoples of the American continents have a long history of textile and fabric use, from the Olmec (1500–400BC) and Aztec (1100–1521)

civilizations in Mexico, to the Paracas (600–175BC) in the Andes, the Incas (1438–1533) in Peru and of course including the Maya in the Yucatán and Central America (2600BC–1700AD). Nowadays, each region still has its own distinctive dress traditions. These vary widely from one ethnic group and community to another, ranging from the *huipil* (a wide, sleeveless tunic for women) in Mexico and Guatemala, to the black, red, green and gold Rastafarian dress of Jamaica, and from the iconic feather headdresses and face and body-painting of Amazonia, to the coca-leaf pouches of Peru and Bolivia.

Before the arrival of the Spanish and the Portuguese, rival native cultures had for centuries been vying for supreme control of the southern continent and the central isthmus. They had also learned and borrowed from each other. The Aztecs of Mexico, for example, drew freely on the cultural legacy of the earlier Toltecs. The conquerors brought many influences with them, not least of which was the

Opposite Model walks the runway for Elie Saab Spring/Summer 2010, Paris Fashion Week Haute Couture

Ecuadorean craftsman weaves a Panama straw hat

Catholic religion, which, along with later evangelical Christian religions, required the covering of the body, a stark conflict in ideology with the natives' nudity or partial nudity. The European colonizers also brought in sheep to provide wool, new technologies (notably the floor or treadle loom) and European garment styles. Gradually, as in other parts of the world where the West had clashed with local populations, European-style clothing eventually replaced indigenous dress in many areas or was combined with pre-Hispanic styles–for example, short pants with tunics in Ecuador.

Perhaps because of the long history of struggle against foreign conquest, there has always been an association in the region between politics and dress. In pre-Conquest times, highly stratified societies such as those of the Inca and the Aztecs imposed strict sumptuary rules on their citizens–for example, the wearing of cotton was forbidden save for the ultra-elite of society. But with the arrival of the Spanish, this order was demolished and cotton,

whose production for export was expanded by the Europeans, became widespread throughout all walks of society. When Spanish rule in Mexico came to an end in 1821, new styles of dress evolved to express the country's nascent sense of nationhood. Similarly, in Guatemala the wearing of *traje*, the clothing worn by descendants of the Maya, has been invested with political meaning and is closely associated with native identity, while in a modern example of the politics of dress in Latin America, Bolivian president Evo Morales wore for his inauguration a specially commissioned brilliant red tunic and four-cornered cap reminiscent of the dress of the pre-Hispanic Tiwanaku elite.

Dress has also been deployed strategically to serve darker political ends. In Chile, after the overthrow of Salvador Allende, uniforms were used to reinforce the authority of the Pinochet regime, both in civil and military contexts, and women were not allowed to don trousers. Citizens of Argentina and Uruguay around this time were also constrained by strict gender codes when it came to clothing. Symbolic dress sometimes projected a vision of resistance to the human rights abuses and violations of the 'Dirty War' in Argentina, which lasted from 1976 to 1983, and the military dictatorship in Uruguay, across a longer period from 1973 to 1985. During the previous decade, after the revolution in Cuba, a penchant for military-inspired Castro hats had also swept the nation.

From the mid-20th century onwards, social revolution in South and Central American countries was often reflected in fashion, with women eventually adopting trousers, the bikini and the miniskirt, and once again the flesh long banned as taboo by the Catholic Church began to emerge from beneath layers of religiously imposed, doctrinally correct clothing. In São Paulo in 1958, a national textile industry fair boasted 97 exhibitors, where fashion designer Zuzu Angel displayed natural-fibre textiles decorated with shells, bamboo and Brazilian stones. Zuzu Angel's embroidered creations, inspired by the *cangaceiros* (a kind of outlaw cast in northeastern Brazil who fought for the poor), were soon worn by international celebrities such as Joan Crawford and Kim Novak and were featured in the windows of prestigious Western retailers such as Bergdorf Goodman in New York City. International celebrities such as Yul Brynner and Gina Lollobrigida flocked to fashionable beach resorts in Punta del Este, Uruguay, in the 1960s, as does today's high-fashion elite. Brazilian fashion shows highlighted the idea of 'Brazilian-ness' – in look, style, and fashion – and invested authenticity in Brazilian fashion products. International fashion from the 1960s also expanded its exotic inventory to include the gaucho look of Argentina, Uruguay and southern Brazil.

Today, Latin America is looking towards the creation of its own self-sufficient fashion industry, drawing on its rich indigenous history as well as its long engagement with Europe to create an aesthetic all of its own. 'Young Latin American women today are very sensual, sexy and have a strong personality,' explained *Vogue Latin America*'s Editor-in-Chief Eva Hughes in 2010. 'They like to travel and are very international, yet they still have a local flair, and are proud of their country.'

Stone skulls on a wall of the Templo Mayor ruins in Mexico City

Armando Mafud
Autumn/Winter
2009,
Mexico City

Mexico

From its dashing charros (cowboys) and breathtaking sweeping desert landscapes to the former decadence of the Mayan and Aztec civilizations – both their peoples and their archaeological remnants – Mexico has enchanted European artists and fashion designers alike since the Spanish first began to conquer it in 1519. Lanvin (Resort 2010), Matthew Williamson (Spring/Summer 2008), Nathan Jenden (Spring/Summer 2008), Nicole Miller (Spring/Summer 2007) and Jean Paul Gaultier (Couture Spring/Summer 2010) are all notable instances of Mexican influence on the runway. Jean Paul Gaultier, for his Spring/Summer 2010 couture show in Paris, indulged in the romance of the traditional charro costume. Models decked in fringed mariachi suits, rebozo-style shawls (common among Mexican women as a covering for the head and shoulders) and topped with sombreros were followed by Amazonian warriors, complete with armour accents in the form of breastplates, clad in Aztec-inspired tribal gowns woven from leaves and shredded palms. Gaultier cited a trip to the British Museum's exhibition about the Aztec emperor Moctezuma in 2009 as the inspiration for the collection. But beyond serving as inspiration for the high-fashion catwalks of Europe and the United States, Mexico is not without fashion icons in its own right. Home to Frida Kahlo, an artist whose unique sense of personal style served not only as inspiration for the designers of her day but also for those of ours, Mexico has long secured its own rightful place in the global fashion hierarchy. In a 1939 visit to Paris, Kahlo was fêted by the world of haute couture to such an extent that the

Illustration of the Aztec sun and warrior god, Tonatiuh

Woman at cemetery during Day of the Dead (Dias de los Muertos) celebration, Teotitlan del Valle, Oaxaca Province, Mexico

Embroidery on a *huipil*, a traditional Mexican dress

globally renowned Italian designer Elsa Schiaparelli designed a dress inspired by her, known as La Robe de Madame Rivera. Soon, Parisiennes aplenty had adopted the look, while French *Vogue* even ran a photograph of Kahlo's hand, laden with its signature chunky cocktail rings, on the cover. In recent times, fashion designers such as Jean Paul Gaultier (1997) have also paid homage to the late icon, offering their own reinterpretations of her famous image on the runways of Paris. In many respects, Frida Kahlo is the perfect fashion ambassador for Mexico, with a style that is eclectic, extremely creative, grounded in interpretation of the local and traditional yet with an idiosyncratic eye towards innovation.

After the arrival of the conquistadores in 1519, Mesoamerican clothing underwent some far-reaching changes as Spanish settlers introduced new materials and textile techniques, as well as the patterns and silhouettes of European tailoring. Indigenous clothing styles, meanwhile, were affected both by the abolition of the old social hierarchy and the imposition of Christianity. The latter was accompanied by the pressure for indigenous men and women, many of whom previously went nude or bare-breasted to abandon the loincloth for trousers, skirts and blouses. The mixing of various races –indigenous Indian, European and African – on Mexican soil produced what the Spaniards regarded as new groups of people (mestizos, mulattos, etc.), whose racial permutations were rigidly classified. Dress became a simple yet effective way of reinforcing the resulting colonial caste system.

With the end of Spanish rule in 1821, New Spain became Mexico. Over the next 90 years, periods of turmoil and economic crisis alternated with brief stretches of political stability. Although the wealthy continued to dress in the European style, two fundamentally and quintessentially Mexican garments achieved widespread popularity with people of all social classes. One was the rebozo, the rectangular shawl which has inspired many

Mexico, Oaxaca, Istmo, portrait of woman
in traditional costume

Hispanic Charro

international designers over the years, including the Paris-based Italian fashion legend Elsa Schiaparelli in the 1940s and Jean Paul Gaultier in the 1990s.

European visitors to Mexico in the 19th century wrote evocative descriptions of the eye-catching clothing worn by the Mexican cowboy, the charro, a figure which has since gone on to romance the world of high fashion alongside its North American counterpart. The riding of horses was an important pastime among wealthy landowners, who spent large sums on their accoutrements, and accordingly a highly stylized charro look was created: embroidered breeches of coloured leather ornamented with silver buttons, a short jacket and an elegant cloak. Elaborately tooled or embroidered leather gaiters were tied over soft leather boots, while hats were large and low-crowned. The female counterpart of the charro was the china poblana, an outfit comprised of a full, wool, peasant-style skirt, a deep upper section of lighter material gathered into a waistband for pleating, and a white

embroidered blouse accessorized with a beaded necklace topped off with a silk *rebozo*. Both the china poblana and charro costume were seen as expressions of national identity, and both live on in Mexican festivals and cinema today.

Frida Kahlo adopted many of the key elements of the china poblana in creating the signature eclectic folk-art-meets-popular-culture looks that catapulted her to fashion fame. In addition to Jean Paul Gaultier, Givenchy's Riccardo Tisci has also fallen under the spell of Kahlo's bohemian mystique, citing her as inspiration for both his Resort 2011 and Autumn/Winter 2010 couture collections. The couture collection even looked to Kahlo's biography and her macabre yet romantic outlook on the world. Referencing her lifelong spinal conditions, zipper detailing came in the shape of bones, while skeleton motifs were rife. In many of her self-portraits she is wearing fringed *rebozos*, floor-length skirts, *huaraches* (a kind of sandal), and other items of regional dress. Her offbeat choice

Model wears
Mexican charro
inspired outfit for
Jean Paul Gaultier
Haute Couture
Spring/Summer
2010, Paris

Model wears
Mexican charro
inspired outfit for
Jean Paul Gaultier
Haute Couture
Spring/Summer
2010, Paris

Frida Kahlo painting

An Oaxacan weaver

cultures and defined her own highly personal style. Her collection included more than 180 garments, many from the state of Oaxaca, but there was one combination that she favoured above all others: the clothing worn by Zapotec women on the Isthmus of Tehuantepec in Oaxaca.

'There are endless opportunities for Mexican designers.'

Tehuana women, widely regarded as sensuous and strong, play a dominant role in Isthmus life, and it was no doubt their poise and courage that appealed so much to Kahlo. Her choice of jewellery was famously eclectic and perhaps sets the precedent for bohemian-style accessorizing today. Although Kahlo delighted in ornate rings, colonial-style pendant earrings, and heavy pre-Columbian jade necklaces, she also wore cheap glass beads at a time when her high-society

peers continued to drape themselves in diamonds, gold and other precious stones. To complement her exotic costumes, Kahlo braided her hair with bright ribbons or decorated it with bows, combs and flowers. The Kahlo look has had considerable impact. As she herself noted with amusement in 1933, 'some of the gringa-women' in New York tried to 'dress a la Mexicana', but without success.

In Mexico today, many fashion designers have taken their inspiration from the nation's textile traditions and cultural heritage. Among them is designer Armando Mafud, born in the historically textile-rich state of Oaxaca, so cherished by Kahlo. He is recognized both within Mexico and internationally for couture collections that capture the essence of his country, the result of his extensive research into 20th-century Mexican culture, including the film industry and various ethnic groups. The widely recognized *huipil* was transformed by Armando Mafud, who narrowed and cropped this traditional woman's top, as well as lengthening the sleeves, and paired it with long, tightly fitted skirts, while maintaining the original style of using appliquéd ribbons to hide the garment's seams.

In 2003, Mexico launched its first fashion week, Días de Moda, sponsored by Mercedes-Benz, the principle backers of New York Fashion Week. The biannual event, which takes place in Mexico City, focuses on Mexico's own most recognized designers, among whom Carlo Demichelis, Ricardo Seco, Elena Gómez Toussaint and César Franco are all names to watch.

'There are endless opportunities for Mexican designers,' Rosalina Villanueva, who works for the trend forecasting company Stylesight, told Fashionista.com in 2010. 'Many are born and raised in Mexico, but do have some other backgrounds rooted in Latin America and Europe. They all have talent and a unique vision. I'm sure they'll be able to start venturing to international fashion weeks and have successes beyond the Mexican borders.'

RECOMMENDED DESIGNERS AND RESOURCES
Mexico

Gianfranco Reni
Ricardo Seco
Alexia Ulibarri

Armando Mafud Autumn/Winter 2009, Mexico City

Armando Mafud Autumn/Winter 2009, Mexico City

Armando
Mafud Autumn/
Winter 2009,
Mexico City

Armando Mafud
Autumn/Winter
2009,
Mexico City

Model wears creation by Mexican designer Elena Gomez Toussaint at Fashion Week 2010, Mexico City

Design by Cesar Franco at Fashion Week 2010, Mexico City

Colombia

Since its beginnings as a Spanish colony, Colombia has demonstrated a great enthusiasm for Western fashion. More recently, over the last few years, the country has sought to carve out a niche for itself in Latin America's emerging fashion industry. With the creation of a project to promote Colombian identity, supported by several governmental organizations, Colombia has sought to bring together fashion designers and traditional craftsmen with the aim of creating an original and strong style unique to the country. The production of most important items of Western apparel in Colombia has been scaled back in the hope of building a new kind of 'national brand' grounded in Colombian cultural heritage. And it seems to be working. Today, Colombia Moda, in Medellín (the largest textile centre in Latin America), is the largest fashion show in Latin America. Held annually, it celebrated its 21st anniversary in July 2010, and is rapidly becoming known internationally as one of the world's most important fashion events.

During the 1950s, a craze for European-style fashion shows, especially charity events, swept through the Colombian elite. Most notable among these events was a 1954 visit from Christian Dior, during which he presented his legendary H collection. Later, in 1966, the 2000 Fashion Show showcased the works of the most famous Colombian artists and designers and was a milestone for Colombian cultural society. Over the years, the creation of national fashion grew as national fashion designers appeared, presenting

Alicia by Amelia Toro on display at Colombia Moda 2010

Alicia by Amelia Toro on display at Colombia Moda 2010

Model wears an Olga Piedrahita design during a Latin American fashion show in Madrid, 2007

Model in leopard
print dress by
Esteban Cortázar
at the opening of
ColombiaModa
2010

their own sartorial interpretations whilst cautiously navigating the parameters of European tailoring. The stand-out designers from the 1950s include Daniel Valdiri and Toby Setton; in the 1960s, Amalín de Hazbún, Marlene Hoffman and the Asociación Colombiana de Alta Costura (the Colombian Haute Couture Association) came to prominence; and in more recent years, those who have made their mark include Álvaro Reyes, Ayerbe & Quintana, Alonso Uribe and John Miranda. In the 1990s, Colombian fashion experienced a considerable boom due to the international success of designers such as Silvia Tcherassi, Hernán Zajar and Olga Piedrahita.

'Women here are the epitome of what a Latin woman represents: flamboyant, sexy, feminine, curvaceous.'

Esteban Cortázar, born in Bogotá as recently as 1984, is the former Creative Director of luxury brand Ungaro, and perhaps Colombia's most famous fashion export. In 2002, Esteban Cortazar's eponymous label made its runway debut to critical acclaim, and in 2003, he managed to coax retired supermodel Cindy Crawford back onto the runway when she agreed to open and close his Spring/Summer 2004 show. In 2007, Esteban Cortázar was installed at the helm at the house of Ungaro, breathing new life into the classic label and drawing praise from critics. However, he famously left in 2009 after American actress Lindsay Lohan was brought on board as a creative consultant, to the dismay of many industry insiders, and the house soon found itself in financial difficulties.

In 2010 Esteban Cortázar made his catwalk comeback when he took up the star position at Colombian Fashion Week, his show kicking off the festival. He showed his new line, a collaboration with Colombian high-street brand éxito, and received rave reviews for reworking his high-octane, cool-girl glamour into an affordable range.

Colombian designer Hernán Zajar with his models during his Spring/Summer 2006 collection, Milan

Design by Colombian designer Hernán Zajar during Colombiatex 2005

Creation by Francesca Miranda, Colombia Moda 2010

Colombian designer Alvaro Reyes showcases at Mexico Fashion Week 2007

'My aim wasn't to work in high-end in Colombia, because that represents a tiny segment of the population that can afford to shop abroad. I wanted to bring international fashion here, to everyone. The challenge was to propose, not dictate, references from Paris and New York, but fit for Colombian women,' he told Fashionista.com in 2010.

In the last few years, marked by events such as Cortázar's return to his homeland, the project to promote Colombian identity has changed both the way people dress in the largest Colombian cities and the way people nationwide think about the aesthetics of dress stemming from the region. The Colombian fashion or 'national brand' that has been created is easy to identify and is widely accepted by Colombians as well as around the world, generating significant sales in international boutiques and projecting a positive and upwardly evolving picture of the country to the fashion world at large. Officially launched in the 2003 at the Colombia Moda fair in Medellín, the project features various handmade products from organizations and haute-couture designers, including the works of the internationally renowned Maria Luisa Ortiz, as well as others by Olga Piedrahita and Lina Cantillo. In 2004, designers such as Hernán Zahar, Pepa Pombo, Maria Elena Villamil and Judy Hazbún took part in the project,

and in 2005, Hernán Zahar, Amelia Toro and Beatriz Camacho jumped on board, followed by, in 2006, Maria Luisa Ortiz and Beatriz Camacho. Soon the Colombian identity initiative was being noticed more widely by the media, by clothing brands, and by designers, artists and pro-handmade organizations, and is now recognized worldwide.

'Women here are the epitome of what a Latin woman represents: flamboyant, sexy, feminine, curvaceous,' Esteban Cortázar told *Interview Magazine* in 2010. 'French women have a totally different body type and culture, and are more exposed to fashion. The idea was to mix those two worlds and bring an aesthetic that might be intimidating for women here to explore. The only way for it to work was for it to be made by a Colombian designer, because they feel they can relate to it.'

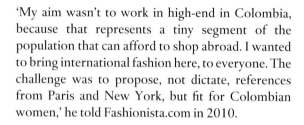

RECOMMENDED DESIGNERS AND RESOURCES
Colombia

Esteban Cortázar
Maria Luisa Ortiz
Olga Piedrahita
Lina Cantillo

Hernán Zahar
Pepa Pombo
Maria Elena Villamil
Judy Hazbún
Amelia Toro
Beatriz Camacho

Colombian
designer
Alvaro Reyes
showcases at
Mexico Fashion
Week 2007

Brazil

It's the land where perfectly proportioned, bronzed, long-limbed beauties the calibre of world famous mega-model Gisele Bündchen *do* grow on trees, the home of *Carnaval* and samba, whose vibrant colours and bright shimmer has inspired a host of designers. But more than just ripe with fashion-ready exports, at home the former Portuguese colony's designers are seeking to construct a notion of Brazilian fashion with designs that probe the essence of what it means to be Brazilian beyond the beaches and the beautiful women. The idea of 'Brazilian-ness' has been a recurrent one in national fashion trends, as designers over the last three decades have sought to understand and explore the multicultural influences at work in their nation. Among those designers with cultural awareness at the top of their design agenda were Glória Coelho and Walter Rodrigues at the beginning of the 1980s, the avant-garde creations of Alexandre Herchcovitch in the 1990s, the innovations of early-21st-century icons Karlla Girotto and Jum Nakao, and finally representations of local cultural roots by Minas Gerais native Ronaldo Fraga.

The creation of a national Brazilian fashion industry dates to the end of the 19th and the beginning of the 20th centuries, when the first fashion magazines were launched in department stores opened across Rio de Janeiro. Mappin department stores opened in central São Paulo in 1913, when the city had only 239,000 inhabitants, compared to the 12 million it has today. At the time only a few stores in São

Opposite Model Gisele Bundchen at Christian Dior's 60th Anniversary show Autumn/Winter 2008 during Paris Haute Couture Fashion Week
Top Models at the end of Ronaldo Fraga's fashion show at Sao Paulo Fashion Week Summer 2011

Design by Walter Rodrigues Autumn/Winter 2011,
Rio de Janeiro

Gloria Coelho Autumn/Winter 2010, Sao Paulo

Paulo and Buenos Aires in neighbouring Argentina sold ready-to-wear clothes, so Mappin was a smash success from the outset. Although economic and cultural nationalism began to prevail throughout Latin America, the Brazilian elite still preferred to attire themselves in the latest designer fashions from Europe to convey their social status. The Mappin stores staged their first fashion showcase in the 1920s, a private show presented in the quintessentially European manner of the tea salon.

Initiatives to establish a national textile industry to support a fledgling fashion industry gained momentum in the 1950s, particularly where cotton was concerned. Bangu in Rio de Janeiro and Matarazzo in São Paulo, both textile companies, sponsored fashion designers such as Jacques Fath, Hubert de Givenchy, Christian Dior, Jean Patou and Jeanne Lanvin, initiating 'fashion festivals' with proceeds going to charity which were gratefully received. In 1958, FENIT, a Brazilian textile

industry fair, was established to unite the textile and emerging fashion industries. With the help of Rhodia, a chemical company that had become closely linked to the fashion industry through the perfume atomizer it invented and marketed in the 1920s, renowned Brazilian fashion designers of the 1960s such as Guilherme Guimarães, José Nunes andAlceu Penna presented collections made of Rhodia's synthetic fabrics that celebrated the idea of 'Brazilian-ness' in fashion.

The development of synthetic fibres in general also helped Brazil put itself on the map as a titan of beach fashion. Modern beachwear and trend-setting garments executed in cutting-edge new fabrics first began appearing on the beaches of Rio de Janeiro in the 1960s, inaugurating a new revolutionary period during which Brazil established itself on the international fashion scene. At this time, the prestigious status of haute couture in general was also transformed, as television and

Gloria Coelho
Autumn/Winter
2010,
Sao Paulo

popular consumption-oriented inventions began to influence the lives of middle-class women. Unisex fashions such as blue jeans and t-shirts helped break down the rigid barriers of sexual and behavioral differentiation typical of so many Latin American countries. The stress on bodily freedom (e.g. the emergence of the notorious Brazilian thong bikini) at the beach could be and was at the time understood to be a form of resistance to the military dictatorship of 1964 to 1985. Unisex thongs and flower-power designs represented, to borrow the words of cultural critic Luiz Carlos Maciel, the only 'free' territory in a staunchly dictatorial country.

In the same vein of fashion as freedom, a generation of young club kids designing avant-garde and conceptually intriguing politically loaded garments in the 1990s fuelled an entire counterculture fashion phenomenon all by themselves. In 1994, the Phytoervas beauty company realized the market potential of this new generation of hip underground designers and created an event specially to showcase their work. By this time, the clubber phenomenon had spread throughout Brazil, and in Recife, a major city on the northeastern coast, techno mix music invaded bars previously dominated by *forró*, a more traditional kind of popular music that originated in the weekly balls and dances landowners put on for farm workers to keep them from migrating to the cities. Bands such as Nação Zumbi, the band formed by the Brazilian singer Chico Science, began to include other traditional rhythms such as *maracatu* and *coco de roda* within the techno beat and dressed in clothing that emphasized Recife's traditional heritage, in particular a kind of local handmade lace called *renascence*; featuring motifs such as pineapples, leaves and flowers, *renascença* originated in Venice, Italy, in the 16th century and arrived in Brazil in the luggage of European nuns, who settled in the rural state of Pernambuco and taught the craft to local women.

Shoes by designer Fause Haten Spring/Summer 2011, Sao Paulo

Model displays a design of FH by Fause Haten
Spring/Summer 2010 at Sao Paulo Fashion Week

Gisele Bundchen for Colcci at Sao Paulo Fashion Week
Summer 2011

Within a few months, the new youth movement, initially called mangue beat, became known throughout the country as mangue fashion, which had emerged on the scene after Recife-born designer Eduardo Ferreira participated in a Phytoervas fashion campaign. Other key designers of mangue fashion include avant-garde club-kid darling Alexandre Herchcovitch (who now shows at New York Fashion Week), Jum Nakao, Ronaldo Fraga, Carla Fincato, Marcelo Sommer, Fause Haten, Mário Queiroz, and Walter Rodrigues. This so-called Phytoervas generation, the stars of São Paulo Fashion Week, not only stimulated the Brazilian fashion industry but enhanced its status on the international scene. By the late 1990s, an official calendar for Brazilian fashion had been established by Morumbi Fashion Brazil, which eventually led to the creation of São Paulo Fashion Week, starring the Phytoervas generation designers, and a string of international superstar models including Gisele Bündchen, Adriana Lima, Alessandra Ambrosio and Carol Trentini.

The establishment of São Paulo Fashion Week in 1996 marked a turning point in the history of national fashion, as this was the first time the most important fashion labels in Brazil had been united together under one banner. It aimed to unify national textile production in order to strengthen, professionalize and showcase Brazilian fashion to the rest of Latin America and the world beyond. Luminosidade, sponsored the fashion week, as a result skyrocketing its founder Paulo Borges to the status of Brazilian fashion super-legend. São Paulo Fashion Week, also called Fashion without Borders, takes place during the Fundação Bienal de São Paulo and has become the place to see shows of the principal Brazilian collections of women's and men's ready-to-wear, as well as leading beach fashions. São Paulo Fashion Week has helped Brazilian designers earn their reputations as audaciously creative in the context of global fashion trends, and in 2009 São Paulo entered the top ten list of most important global fashion capitals, clocking in at number 8. In fact, fashion editorial legends Isabella Blow and Suzy Menkes of The International Herald Tribune at

Carlos Miele
Spring/Summer
2011,
New York

the time dubbed São Paulo Latin America's fashion capital, outshining neighbouring fashion centres such as Bogotá and Buenos Aires.

In recent years, Brazilian television has seen a surge in press coverage of national fashion design. By 2009, national media coverage of São Paulo Fashion Week had surpassed that of any other event except soccer. Today, Brazil boasts more than 50 fashion education programmes, concentrated in the southeastern region of the country and offering a healthy variety of courses in topics ranging from fashion theory and journalism to design at both undergraduate and postgraduate levels. Each year, these programmes see approximately 8,000 students graduate, and generate close to US $35 million in revenue.

The Brazilian fashion phenomenon has led to the development of a strong identity on the global style scene. Overwhelmed by her pride in her country,

the Brazilian model Mariana Weickert (who has modelled for the likes of Alexander McQueen, Louis Vuitton, Versace, Marc Jacobs and Armani) infamously branded her lower back with the phrase, 'Made in Brazil', sending shock waves throughout the fashion industry, where non-tattooed models are not only the norm but the staunch rule, but epitomizing the local sentiment about embracing all things Brazilian. President Luiz Inácio Lula da Silva and his wife Marisa insisted on wearing clothes by Brazilian designers at the inauguration ceremony in 2003. Walter Rodrigues designed three dresses for First Lady Marisa Letícia Lula da Silva, who chose one in the vibrant red of the Workers' Party that she and her husband represent. Her accessories were equally Brazilian, from a golden, rose-shaped brooch to earrings made by renowned jeweller Antonio Bernardo and priced at US $3,500. Renowned Brazilian menswear designer Ricardo Almeida created the president's inauguration suit.

Ronaldo Fraga Spring/Summer 2011, Sao Paulo

Jum Nakao Spring/Summer 2005, Sao Paulo

Jum Nakao
Spring/Summer
2005,
Sao Paulo

Jum Nakao
Spring/Summer
2005,
Sao Paulo

Alexandre Herchcovitvh Autumn/Winter 2010, New York

Alexandre Herchcovitvh Spring/Summer 2011, New York

The idea of fashion 'made in Brazil' has proved to be more than a brand of 'Brazilian-ness' to be listed under luxury goods for export. Fashion in Brazil challenges stereotypes and constantly reinvents the meaning of Brazilian features, according to São Paulo Fashion Week founder Paulo Borges. In an interview published in Brazilian *Elle*, he remarked that he did not believe in making clothes for Brazilian people or clothes with a Brazilian style. A nationally manufactured fashion, however, generates employment and creates a space for collective memory and desire while remaining distinct from folkloric stereotypes. His comment reflects the grounding of Brazilian fashion in the fertile soil of culture, national identity and social change. And this is the base from which many top Brazilian designers operate today; Ronald Fraga and the highly successful and now New York-based Carlos Miele, in particular, have invested the design process with socially conscious and

environmentally sustainable practices Brazilian dress, body image and culture remain inextricably linked to constructions of national identity and the dynamics of everyday life, but its contribution to global fashion far exceeds the donation of endless bevies of Brazilian beauties, being something with a commitment to society and culture that is hard to find anywhere else in the fashion world.

RECOMMENDED DESIGNERS AND RESOURCES
Brazil

Lucas Nascimento
Melk Z-Da
Mara Mac label

(Mara MacDowell)
Alexandre Herchcovitch
Sao Paulo Fashion Week
http://ffw.com.br/spfw/

Argentina

Once roamed by the legendary gauchos, whose cropped, flared-leg, trademark trousers have taken many a turn down the runway over the years, Argentina is the birthplace of one of Latin America's most famous fashion icons, the Dior-clad former First Lady Eva Perón. Her legacy of high fashion and glamour, despite the years of political darkness that accompanied it, is somewhat emblematic of the country's long established and prolific fashion industry: at once poised and at home with the precedents of European tailoring and fashions, but with a certain Argentinian twist. Moreover, the political tensions Eva Perón and her couture wardrobe represented reflect Argentinian fashion's intimate connections with the national culture, with citizenship and with social change.

European explorers arrived in what is now Argentina in 1516, with the Spanish founding the permanent colony of Buenos Aires in 1580. The Argentinians won their independence from the Spanish in 1818, and a modern Argentinian textile manufacturing industry emerged from the semi-industrial colonial workshops, known as *obrajes*. In colonial times, Buenos Aires had served as the port epicentre, and a number of provider cities such as Catamarca, Salta, Corrientes, Santiago del Estero, Tucumán and Córdoba developed their textile manufacture of

Semilllero UBA Spring/Summer 2011 at Buenos Aires Fashion Week, 2010

Eva Peron, 1940

wool, cotton, silk, and hemp fibres. The establishment of the free trade policy of 1778 and the creation of a customs system at the borders and ports in 1781 prepared the way for a new economic model. This was how the European colonial powers tended to support their own exports to colonies, which the Spanish Crown implemented to support its own products, but which instead wound up paving the way for the industrialized production of fashion to spring up alongside the burgeoning textile industry.

In 1946 General Juan Perón was elected president. His wife, Eva Duarte Perón, had emerged from poverty, and went on to steal the affections of the people of both her own country and the world. Playing a central political role in her husband's administration until her untimely death in 1952, Eva Peron won huge support amongst her country's poor, her so-called *descamisados* (literally 'shirtless ones'), thanks to the Eva Perón Foundation and the Peronist Women's Party, which she founded after women were granted the right to vote. In a bid to charm the world beyond Argentina's borders, Eva basked in all the fashion fineries a first lady could dream up. Decking herself out in Dior and Chanel as well as the clothes of the best Argentinian designers, even daring to be the first Argentinian woman to don trousers, she was loathed by the upper class for the hypocrisy of dressing in such luxury whilst building her political career upon the love of the poor. Their dislike of her was so intense that many Argentinian fashion designers had to disguise the fact that they dressed her for fear of enraging and alienating their other high-society clients.

After her premature death from cancer at the age of 33, Eva Perón became a figure of fascination around the world, even more than when she was alive. A beautiful romantic heroine, a style icon, by the late 20th century Perón had become the subject of books, plays, even a musical, *Evita*, whose leading role Madonna famously took on in a major Hollywood film of the 1990s. The public's interest in Evita's story naturally translated into an interest in her legendary style, and her classically elegant look has served as a talisman of Argentinian grace for half a century. Most recently, in 2010 Argentinian designer Jorge Ibañez showcased a collection entitled Evita, entirely inspired by the legendary First Lady, to commemorate Argentina's bicentennial.

Alexander Wang Spring/Summer 2009, New York

But a style icon such as Eva Perón does not merely spring out of a desert of fashion design – that is to say, thanks to Argentina's flourishing arts and cultural scene and relative affluence, by the time Eva Perón first addressed her *descamisados* from atop the Casa Rosada (the presidential palace), a highly evolved tradition of fashion design and a host of local designers were already firmly in place, ready and waiting to serve.

Mary Tapia, one of Argentina's most prominent designers, emerged on the fashion scene in the 1960s. Disenchanted with having to wait six months for the latest European fashions to reach Argentinian shores, she refused merely to imitate styles imported from the faraway fashion epicentres, and instead set about pioneering a distinctly Argentinian attitude to design. Her first collection, launched in 1969 and entitled Pachamama prêt-à-porter, utilized the delicate productions of the indigenous peoples of the Colla and Zuleta communities and of Paraguayan women, all of whom were known for creating ponchos, tapestries, and intricately embroidered garments. According to Tapia, the collection revealed textures based on weavings from Otavalo, a town in northern Ecuador, and tapestries from the Ecuadorian capital Quito.

Other designers have expressed facets of national identity in their work. Susana Saulquin has drawn inspiraton from the work of Paco Jamandreu, who presented a glamorous 'gaucho look' collection in New York in 1969 and 1970; and Juan Risuleo developed the concept of 'Argentinian clothes' in the late 1960s. During the struggle between Peronists and anti-Peronists which characterized the country's politics in the 1960s and 1970s, alternative cultural forms flourished amidst the government's repressive practices. From 1976 to 1983, a 'Dirty War' targeted Argentina's own citizens. The regime of Jorge Rafael Videla in particular was responsible for the disappearance of approximately 30,000 people whom the military labelled as subversives. These people, the *desaparecidos* or disappeared, were kidnapped and then executed, with little or no information given as to the whereabouts of their remains and no comfort or relief provided to grieving families. Creatives in all art forms began to register artistically the dynamics of collective identity and everyday life,

Alexander Wang Spring/Summer 2009, New York

and by the early 1980s, a group of young people referred to as the *modernos* or the 'modern crowd', had emerged. Fabricio Forastelli, an Argentinian cultural critic, commented that his first memories of fashion date back to the 1970s, precisely the moment when fashion became *moda.*

Following Argentina's transition to democracy in 1983, young artists and intellectuals in their twenties sought to assert their visions of cultural independence after dictatorship. As a result of the First Biennial of Youth Art, which incorporated catwalk shows into the Bolivia, Garage Argentino and other nightclubs, a new generation of young designers such as Sergio de Loof came to feel that the hauntings of their nation's past seemed as inescapable as they were almost unbearable, and manifested this sentiment in their works. For example, Sergio de Loof's response was to use the transformative power of fashion to escape the trauma of history. In the 1990s, when tabloid magazines like *Gente* and *Caras* featured the exuberant lifestyles of the rich and famous to the chagrin of the general population, marking the perpetually widening gulf between the wealthy and the working class, a few designers turned to the past to expose the nation's dead, the emigrations of political dissenters and its unresolved conflicts to express their outrage. The so-called *Movida Porteña* (or Buenos Aires Scene) was a term derived from *La Movida Madrileña*, which described the hedonistic culture of youth in the Spanish capital in the years following the death of General Franco. In Argentina, the movement spread into areas like design, video, comic art and fashion. In fashion, Jean Paul Gaultier (in particular his deconstructive take on fashion history), Claude Montana and Spanish designer Sybilla became extremely influential for the new crop of socially conscious Argentinian designers. The final collections of the biennial showcased the collections of Gabriel Grippo, Gaby Bunader and others.

After 1989 and during the 1990s, Sergio de Loof emerged at the head of this new politically informed fashion pack. In June 1989, his collection Latina Winter by Cotolengo Fashion recycled and reconfigured second-hand garments from the Salvation Army. Self-proclaimed 'poor geniuses' Gabriel Grippo, Andrés Baño, Gaby Bunader and

Kelo Romero launched what became known as 'poverty fashion', through proposals that explored the aesthetics of urban subculture (in this case, the poor, transvestites, Bolivian day labourers and the unemployed) yet treated the subjects with a dose of ironic superficiality.

'Clothing was a martyr.'

An impoverished look has been a theme in fashion since the emergence of the deliberately austere clothes of Japanese designers like Yohji Yamamoto and also Rei Kawakubo, for her label Comme des Garçons, in the early 1980s. This apocalyptic vision of clothing and dress, in addition to its deconstructionist point of view, strongly influenced Argentinian fashion in the late 1980s and helped seal the nation's place amongst the world's bastions of the avant-garde, along with other strongholds such as Antwerp and Tokyo. Economic crisis impacted Argentinian fashion deeply, with poverty and unemployment becoming the unavoidable realities of daily life for many people. This notion of 'poverty chic' still translates to runways today, especially since the 2008 collapse of the global economic system, following which brands such as Prada's Miu Miu offered hole-ridden collections in drab fabrics. A resurrection of the grunge trend of the 1990s swept across catwalks as recently as 2009/10 as a new wave of designers, including Alexander Wang and Rag & Bone. looked to the hipster grunge scene of urban youth for catwalk inspiration.

Marcelo Serna Spring/Summer 2011 at Buenos Aires Fashion Week, 2010

One of the most interesting figures on the Buenos Aires fashion scene in recent decades was Kelo Romero (1962–2006). Like Sergio de Loof and Gabriel Grippo, Kelo Romero had focused on the ability of fashion design to recast cheap nothings and textile remnants into new objects with conceptual and artistic value, thus creating what was called *sudaca* fashion, or deconstructionist forms for denim. *Sudaca* is a pejorative term used in Spain to refer to Latin American immigrants seeking employment and opportunity there. Kelo Romero stated that his work 'exceeded the message imparted by the fabric', because he was highly critical of the notion of clothes necessarily having to take on a certain form and utilize the same basic colour palette. 'Clothing was a martyr,' he declared, as people used it to protect themselves, conceal their faces with masks, and lump themselves into groups. Romero's designs were a mixture of these recycled materials and items such as precious pearls and luxurious fabrics, a bringing together of the low and high cultures of Buenos Aires, a vision that included all the strata of Argentinian society.

This same tension played itself out in the catwalk spaces chosen by many of these designers. While the Bolivia and Garage Argentino clubs provided the initial catwalks, there was a dream-like and almost escapist space for designers at El Dorado nightclub. Almost in defiance of the economic crisis, de Loof recalls, owners of fashion magazines, undercover businesspeople, the press and the designers sat in a corner drinking champagne and being photographed. He felt that this moment was like 'a second phase of sweet silver', a reference to the meaning of Argentina's name, the 'land of silver'. He could not remember another time when there had been so much money on hand. During the

Creation by Miuccia Prada for Miu Miu
Spring/Summer 2009, Paris

Creation by Miuccia Prada for Miu Miu
Spring/Summer 2009, Paris

presidency of Carlos Menem (1989–99), exhibitions of populist-style frivolity were commonly referred to as 'pizza with champagne'.

It was during the 1990s that deconstruction, as inspired by the late 20th-century philosophy of Jacques Derrida, became an exercise in fashion design programmes at the University of Buenos Aires and other institutions, such as the Centro de Artes Visuales design school and the technological institute ORT Argentina. The design syllabuses of new universities such as the University of Palermo were also inspired by architecture, by fashion designers who studied at the Antwerp Royal Academy of Arts (among them Martin Margiela, Dries Van Noten and Ann Demeulemeester), by the designs of Yohji Yamamoto and Rei Kawakubo, and by vintage clothing.

Contemporary political struggles in Argentina have brought about significant shifts in the way fashion is designed, consumed and understood. While Argentinian fashion in the 1990s drew inspiration from the declining textile industry, the creative designs of those responding to the influx of global goods and the boom that occurred in the new century transformed culture and the economy. Following devaluation of the Argentinian peso, the textile sector emerged as one of the fastest-growing industries in the nation, with a 320% increase in the number of fashion boutiques in the years from 1994 to 2003, according to a Buenos Aires government study of economic development. As new fashion districts, including Palermo Viejo and San Telmo, emerged in the heart of Buenos Aires, uniquely Argentinian products began to feature in museums and fashion magazines worldwide. Responding to this phenomenon, the Buenos Aires city government began to subsidize fashion by circulating maps to tourists wishing to locate up-and-coming design studios.

In 2002, Pablo Ramírez, one of Argentina's most renowned designers, presented his collection Patria in homage to all educators whose contributions have led to freedom. The winter collection, which received a standing ovation, presented classical-style clothes inspired by the 19th century, including lapels inlaid with Swarovski crystals and Phrygian caps that resonated with the spirit of Argentinian independence heroes. Pablo Ramírez remembered as the source of his inspiration the days of 19th and 20th of December 2001, when he was in Belgrano on a bus that changed its route because demonstrators were burning tires at the Cabildo, the building in downtown Buenos Aires from which the Spanish colonial powers had ruled. Suddenly he saw a man coming out of one of the fine homes in Belgrano to set up loudspeakers on the street to play the national anthem. This gesture moved him so much that he experienced the birth, or more accurately the rebirth, of his own patriotism.

The cultural momentum of the Buenos Aires fashion scene had long been studied with great interest by city government officials. The Metropolitan Design Centre was established while Fernando de La Rúa was the mayor of the city; following his election as the country's president in 1999, the Ministry of Culture co-sponsored events such as Buenos Aires never sleeps, which included massive catwalk shows on the front stairs of the University of Buenos Aires Law School, with supermodels Claudia Schiffer, Naomi Campbell and Valeria Mazza, and established new design awards. That same year, the Grupo Pampa launched Buenos Aires Fashion Week, which both energized and competed with other events such as Buenos Aires Alta Moda (Buenos Aires Haute Couture) and the Paseo Alcorta Fashion Week. In Argentina today, the fashion scene relies heavily on one-of-a-kind creations, commonly referred to as 'auteur designs', in the trendy neighbourhoods of Palermo and San Telmo. Far from the silhouette of the tango as projected in Hollywood films and global culture, the contemporary designs of Argentina continue to reveal avant-garde visions and political tensions, and a cultural history that is continuously being remade as the country remakes itself.

RECOMMENDED DESIGNERS AND RESOURCES
Argentina

Pablo Ramirez
Victor de Souza
Jorge Ibanez

Marcelo Sanra Trosman
Buenos Aires Fashion Week
http://www.bafweek.com/
Ans: Beauties' Dealer – Blog
http://anslatindesigns.blogspot.com/

Cuban woman in traditional dress

Cuba

Cuba is one of the largest islands of the Caribbean, with its capital Havana being founded by Spanish colonizers in 1519. Since then, the city has served as one of the most important ports for Latin America as a whole. A nexus for trade, Spanish and other European ships always brought with them to Cuban shores shoes and apparel of all kinds to meet the demand of colonial aristocrats and merchants. In turn, European styles were imitated and then altered to produce original Cuban clothing that matched the needs of the locals in the humid tropical climate. In 1902, Cuba became an independent nation, and for the next six decades, until the Revolution of 1959, American and European clothes were worn partly as a source of inspiration to produce local apparel. Dramatic changes occurred when international economic exchange came to a halt and the influx of foreign clothes and models was stopped.

The Revolution in Cuba changed the way people lived. At the end of 1959, when Fulgencio Batista, the Cuban President, fled the country, the economy fell completely into the hands of the private sector. With the arrival of Fidel Castro, private property was gradually nationalized, while in 1960 the Cuban government nationalized department stores, manufacturing plants, warehouses, banks, insurance companies, sugar mills and private health clinics. Because the nationalization process did not happen overnight, for a time fashion retailers were able to continue to meet the demands of their clientele, who had acquired a taste for the latest American and European trends. In reaction to the Revolution and to Cuba's alliance with the Soviet Union, in 1962 the United States imposed an embargo against Cuba, which continues to this day.

A t-shirt with a portrait of Che Guevara

By 1968 the Cuban state was in charge of all industry, including all retail trade and clothing stores. In order to ensure a consistent distribution of goods, the government had established a national rationing system which instituted monthly physical shares of consumer goods such as clothing, food and personal products for each citizen. Therefore, the fashion revolution of the mid-1960s that swept much of the rest of the world was little felt in Cuba. Women wore citrus-coloured sleeveless dresses, as well as slip blouses and dresses. Tiny hipster skirts made of transparent fabrics and little dresses or shorts made of nylon were often what were supplied. Jeans and khakis were available for both males and females, but supply was never able to meet the demand. At the workplace most people wore navy or white and brown uniforms composed of simple cotton skirts or trousers and sport shirts. Dress mass production was possible, of course, with the aid of, and trade with, the Soviet Union, which supplied Cuba with machinery to produce textiles.

Cuba had its worst economic crisis between 1991 and 1995 after the collapse of the Soviet Union (one of the country's main oil suppliers). This period is known as the *período especial*, an economic depression due to shortages of energy resources in the form of petrol and oil derivatives. As a result, the decline in production of basic necessities such as food left Cuban society almost on the verge of starvation. As far as clothing was concerned, the shortage was such that people had to scrap the idea of acquiring new clothes and instead continue to wear their old garments rather than buying new ones–fashion, as it were, ground to a halt. The clothing industry was radically reduced, and the large group of skilled workers who had once worked in the industry found themselves at once unemployed and unable to transfer their skills into other sectors of the economy that were still afloat. Designers, dressmakers and tailors lacked materials to produce their goods, and even sewing at home became almost impossible due to the scarcity of materials. People took to using sheets, bedspreads, tablecloths, and even large rags to make clothes at home.

By the year 2000, however, Cuban fashion was almost back in tune with the rest of the world. Even though the US embargo prohibits American businesses from trading or conducting business in or with Cuba, clothes designed and produced using American capital slowly but surely have made their way to the island and re-infused the streets of Havana with fresh fashions. The Cuban fashion item par excellence is the *guayabera*, a kind of men's shirt, and new designers have added new designs to the already rich repertoire. *Guayaberas* in colours never seen before – for instance, red, orange, yellow or pink – are part of more recent collections and were instant hits with the public. In addition, long *guayaberas* for women, worn as a casual dress, evolved from the typical men's garment. Another item that has become a source of national pride, also recognized throughout the world, is the Che Guevara t-shirt, a garment portraying the Argentinian-born Marxist revolutionary hero Ernesto 'Che' Guevara's famous visage. The image, instantly recognized round the world, and donned by countless international would-be hipsters, originated from a photograph of Guevara snapped by Cuban photographer Alberto Korda. Over the years, Cuban designers have created and recreated the Che Guevara t-shirt in all sorts of colours and shapes.

In Havana today there exists an elegant fashion house called La Maison, owned by the Cuban government since its establishment in 1984. Surprisingly, La Maison hosts a fashion show every night of the year, exhibiting its latest fashions alongside selected foreign and Cuban designers. La Maison's headquarters is a mansion decorated in the most exquisite late 19th-century French décor, and boasts a boutique where people can buy mostly Cuban designer clothes. Isabel Toledo, wife of renowned artist Ruben Toledo, is perhaps the most famous Cuban designer active on the international scene today. Born in Camajuani las Villas, she emigrated to the United States together with her family in the late 1960s, then proceeded to study at both New York's prestigious Fashion Institute of Technology and Parsons School of Design. Isabel Toledo debuted in New York in 1985 and most

Opposite Michelle Obama wearing outfit by Cuban designer Isabel Toledo at her husband's inauguration

Cuban models present creations by Rocco Barrocco at his show in Havana, 2008

recently dressed American First Lady Michelle Obama in a lemon-yellow wool dress/overcoat combination for the inauguration of her husband, President Barack Obama.

So while Cuba, still partly shut off from the Western fashion powers that be, still has a way to go before claiming parity with some of its Latin American neighbours in terms of local fashion design and production, its contributions to the wider fashion industry have not been insignificant. Cuba lacks neither creativity nor its own unique sense of style; it is merely a matter of continuing to overcome economic hardships which impact the way people both design and consume fashion. Despite these limitations, originality still thrives, both at home and abroad, and the potential for a dynamic and creative Cuban fashion scene to flourish hovers on the horizon as the country rebuilds.

RECOMMENDED DESIGNERS AND RESOURCES
Cuba

Isabel Toledo
Havana Fashion House
'La Maison'

Puerto Rico

Puerto Rican dress is the result of a convergence of cultures: the native Taínos, the colonizing Spaniards and the African slaves. From the Taínos, the early inhabitants of the island, to its current population, music and dance have enjoyed a privileged position in Puerto Rican society, a popularity accorded to no other art form, including fashion. Thus Puerto Rican dress is inextricable from the cultural phenomenon of Puerto Rican types of dance. Types of dance attributed to the territory most famously include salsa, but the creation of reggaeton is also contested between Panama and Puerto Rico. Dress practices related to all of these dances have somehow influenced all walks of Puerto Rican fashion, from street style to cultural influences to catwalk.

Unlike all the other Latin American countries colonized by Spain, Puerto Rico has never been an independent nation. The island became an American territory as a result of the Spanish–American War of 1898 and was officially named Estado Libre Asociado de Puerto Rico (Freely Associated State

Alexander McQueen
Spring/Summer 2004, Paris

Alexander McQueen
Spring/Summer 2004, Paris

of Puerto Rico) in 1952. After Puerto Ricans were granted US citizenship in 1917, an exodus to the mainland resulted in nearly two-fifths of the total population living in the United States. Fighting to remain faithful to their roots, Puerto Ricans on the mainland have employed music and dance as symbols of national identity and have influenced American rhythms and clothing styles associated with urban and pop music.

Salsa, whose romance has captivated designers such as Alexander McQueen and Christian Dior, has enjoyed great popularity among Puerto Ricans since its inception in the 1960s, though its true origins are often contested between Puerto Rico and Cuba. As with other musical forms, dress styles associated with salsa have evolved with the music itself. During its early days, performers such as Hector Lavoe and Willie Colón carefully crafted the image of well-groomed bad boys, donning partially unbuttoned fitted shirts revealing just a bit of the chest, tailored vests and tight dress trousers in white, black or powder blue. They also accessorized with expensive jewellery and capped off their coordinated looks with Panama hats. Puerto Rican salsa fans, known as *cocolos*, emulated clothing styles worn by their idols, particularly at the height of salsa popularity during the 1970s and 1980s. Men wore sunglasses, tropical printed shirts, dark dress trousers and gold jewellery, while women wore tightly fitted and revealing dresses. Salsa allows dancers to create a sensual spectacle with their dance moves and attire, and both the music and the clothing that developed to accompany it were further commercialized and ever more highly sexualized as its rhythm spread round the world.

Personal appearance is of great importance to most Puerto Ricans, who strive to create a clean well-groomed look incorporating innovative styles. Local fashion designers have been able to compete successfully with international design houses. Among the most prominent Puerto Rican designers are Fernando Pena, Carlota Alfaro, Lisa Thon, Harry Robles, Edgardo Bonilla, Stella Nolasco, Sonia Rivera, Nono Maldonado and Verona.

The establishment of large ex-patriot Puerto Rican communities in New York City resulted in the creation of the term *Nuyorican*, referring to people of Puerto Rican descent born in the New York metropolitan area. Many influential figures have emerged from the *Nuyorican* community including Jennifer Lopez, who as a singer/performer-turned-fashion designer (she launched her successful line JLo in 2001) epitomizes the Puerto Rican relationship between dance and fashion.

RECOMMENDED DESIGNERS AND RESOURCES *Puerto Rico*	
Fernando Pena	Lisa Thon
Carlota Alfaro	Harry Robles
	Edgardo Bonilla
	Stella Nolasco
	Sonia Rivera
	Nono Maldonado
	Verona

Salsa dancers

Model walks the runway at the J-LO fashion show at Fashion Week Miami Beach 2006

Further Reading

Suggested Websites: Blogs, Magazines and more from around the world

Africa

http://onenigerianboy.blogspot.com/
http://www.bellanaija.com/
http://www.arisemagazine.net/
http://naijaholic.blogspot.com/
http://mariankihogo.com/
http://themusingsofondolady.blogspot.com/
http://www.hautefashionafrica.com/
http://nuheila.blogspot.com/
http://vogueprincessnaija.wordpress.com/
http://www.capetowngirl.co.za/
http://www.gq.co.za/
http://lallalydia.blogspot.com/
http://welovehijab.com
http://fashionthreadsblog.com/
http://www.fustany.com
http://www.elle.co.za/

Asia

http://bryanboy.typepad.com/
http://www.thebaghagdiaries.com/
http://www.stylites.net/
http://fashionesedaily.com/
http://styleiris.blogbus.com/
http://www.wodeyichu.com/space/iam_smallfry
http://fashionthreadsblog.com/
http://www.fashiondes.com/
http://www.vogue.com.cn/
http://styleshanghai.i.ph/
http://www.ellechina.com/
http://www.marieclairechina.com/
http://www.chinacandycouture.com/
http://beneaththecrystalstars.blogspot.com/
http://www.japanesestreets.com/
http://www.fashioninjapan.com/
http://japanesefashionstyle.blogspot.com/
http://www.tokyoshoes.com/blog/
http://harajukus.blogspot.com/
http://www.vogue.co.jp/
http://www.elle.co.jp/
http://www.nylon.jp/index.html
http://www.gqjapan.jp/index.html
http://j-walkblog.com/index.php?/weblog/posts/
japanese_fashion/
http://tokyofashiondaily.blogspot.com/
http://www.style.co.kr/vogue
http://elle.atzine.com/elle/elleweb_main.iht
http://www.marieclairekorea.com/user/main/index.asp
http://kokokoreano.com/
http://www.style.co.kr/gq/
http://www.koreanfashiononline.com/
http://korean-fashion.tumblr.com/
http://www.manilafashionobserver.com/

http://stylefromtokyo.blogspot.com/
http://indiafashion123.blogspot.com/
http://sareedreams.com/
http://www.fashiontrendsindia.com/
http://www.vogue.in/
http://www.fashion-bombay.com/
http://wearabout.wordpress.com/

Middle East

http://www.hijabstyle.co.uk/
http://myfashdiary.blogspot.com/
http://fashistanbuller.blogspot.com/
http://www.thestreetswalker.com/
http://israblog.nana10.co.il/tblogread.asp?blog=387973
http://fashistanbuller.blogspot.com/
http://www.confashionsfromkuwait.com/
http://www.dubaisitgirl.com/
http://milkandhoneyimports.com/blog/
http://www.hautemimi.com/
http://www.harpersbazaararabia.com/
(Harpers Bazaar Arabia)
http://fastidiousness.blogspot.com/
http://www.fashion-hermit.com/
http://www.vogue.com.tr/
http://district-h.blogspot.com/
http://www.hellwafashion.com/
http://www.urbansouq.com/
http://www.butterhotshoes.com/
http://www.chicmaryam.com/
http://www.mahryska.com/
http://www.lylalovesfashion.com/
http://fashiongossip10.blogspot.com/
http://outrechic.blogspot.com/
http://istanbulstreetstyle.blogspot.com/
http://istanbulfashionaddict.blogspot.com/
http://lebfashion.blogspot.com/

Latin America

http://thechicmuse.blogspot.com/
http://www.stylescrapbook.com/
http://fashionspotmexico.blogspot.com/
http://www.diariodefiestas.blogspot.com/
http://messthisdress.blogspot.com/
http://madeinbrazil.typepad.com/
http://vogue.mx/
http://www.voguelatam.com/
http://rarascoincidenciasneoyorquinas.blogspot.com/
http://franklincollaodiary.blogspot.com/
http://fashioncoolture.com.br/
http://www.instintodevestir.com/
http://inspiracaofashion.wordpress.com/
http://www.lejeanshere.blogspot.com/

Index